Dialogues on
Relativism, Absolutism, and Beyond

New Dialogues in Philosophy

A series in dialogue form, explicating foundational problems in the philosophy of existence, knowledge, and value

Series Editor
Professor Dale Jacquette
Senior Professorial Chair in Theoretical Philosophy
University of Bern, Switzerland

In the tradition of Plato, Berkeley, Hume, and other great philosophical dramatists, Rowman & Littlefield presents an exciting new series of philosophical dialogues. This innovative series has been conceived to encourage a deeper understanding of philosophy through the literary device of lively argument in scripted dialogues, a pedagogic method that is proven effective in helping students to understand challenging concepts while demonstrating the merits and shortcomings of philosophical positions displaying a wide variety of structure and content. Each volume is compact and affordable, written by a respected scholar whose expertise informs each dialogue, and presents a range of positions through its characters' voices that will resonate with students' interests while encouraging them to engage in philosophical dialogue themselves.

Titles

J. Kellenberger, *Moral Relativism: A Dialogue* (2008)
Michael Ruse, *Evolution and Religion: A Dialogue* (2008)
Charles Taliaferro, *Dialogues about God* (2008)
Brian Orend, *On War: A Dialogue* (2008)
Dale Jacquette, *Dialogues on the Ethics of Capital Punishment* (2009)
Bradley Dowden, *The Metaphysics of Time: A Dialogue* (2009)
Michael Krausz, *Dialogues on Relativism,*
Absolutism, and Beyond: Four Days in India (2011)

Forthcoming Titles

Dan Lloyd, *Ghosts in the Machine: A Dialogue*

Dialogues on
Relativism, Absolutism, and Beyond

Four Days in India

Michael Krausz

ROWMAN & LITTLEFIELD PUBLISHERS, INC.
Lanham • Boulder • New York • Toronto • Plymouth, UK

Published in the United States of America
A wholly owned subsidiary of The Rowman & Littlefield Publishing Group, Inc.
4501 Forbes Boulevard, Suite 200, Lanham, Maryland 20706
http://www.rowmanlittlefield.com

Estover Road, Plymouth PL6 7PY, United Kingdom

British Library Cataloguing in Publication Information Available

Library of Congress Cataloging-in-Publication Data

Krausz, Michael.
    Dialogues on relativism, absolutism, and beyond : four days in India / Michael Krausz.
        p. cm. — (New dialogues in philosophy)
    Includes bibliographical references (p.   ) and index.
    ISBN 978-0-7425-6032-1 (cloth : alk. paper) — ISBN 978-0-7425-6033-8 (pbk. : alk. paper) — ISBN 978-1-4422-0930-5 (electronic)
    1. Relativity. 2. Absoute, The. 3. Philosophy, Indic. I. Title.
    BD221.K73 2011
    149—dc22

                                                                  2010044599

∞™ The paper used in this publication meets the minimum requirements of American National Standard for Information Sciences—Permanence of Paper for Printed Library Materials, ANSI/NISO Z39.48-1992.

Printed in the United States of America

Contents

~

Prologue

Ronnie, Adam, Barbara, and Nina are old friends from their days at Canaday College, where they were all philosophy majors. They had often spoken about their dream one day to visit India together.

After ten years, Ronnie is a professor of anthropology at Canaday College. Adam is a geologist at the National Bureau of Standards in Washington, D.C. Barbara is a psychotherapist at Jefferson Hospital in Philadelphia, and Nina lives in a Hindu (Advaita) ashram in India.

Now they have finally fulfilled their dream. The group has gathered on the veranda of the Ganges View Hotel, overlooking the Ganges River in Varanasi, the holy city of the Hindus. As they drink tea, they are reflecting upon their early morning experience on the boat that took them up the Ganges, where they had viewed the funeral pyres, at which the dead are cremated.

These four friends are fictional. Their names signal their views: Ronnie is a relativist. Adam is an absolutist. Barbara is both. And Nina is neither. Barbara seeks to embrace features of both relativism and absolutism. Nina seeks to go beyond absolutism and relativism. She is a meditator and a mystic. She thinks that beyond Ronnie, Adam, and Barbara's aim for truth is a deeper aim, which is self-realization.

For their helpful suggestions, the author thanks Elizabeth D. Boepple, John Gibson, Dale Jaquette, Christine Koggel, Joyce Lussier, V.A. Rao, Andreea Ritivoi, Jill Stauffer, Bharath Vallabha, Mary Wiseman, David Wong, and students at Bryn Mawr College. For their instruction and inspiration, the author thanks Tenzin Gyatso (the Dalai Lama), Lobsang Gyatso, Ngawang Samten, Swami Shyam, Aatma Shakti, and Jitendra Mohanty.

~

Relativism versus Absolutism:
A First Encounter

The Baby in the Ganges

Adam: Ronnie, when you told me to look over the side of the boat early this morning, I couldn't believe my eyes. I was shocked.

Ronnie: Yes, when I first saw it, I was shocked too.

Adam: At first, it looked like debris floating on the surface of the Ganges. But gradually I realized that it was a dead baby floating on the Ganges!

Barbara: Yes, it was shocking. But you know what? Maybe it wasn't all that shocking after our nice hotel manager Mr. Shashank explained it to me when I returned to the hotel. He could see that the whole thing upset me. He said that such things happen sometimes, and his Western guests are often taken aback. But actually, it is something Indians take in their stride.

Adam: In their stride? How bizarre. What did he say?

Barbara: He explained that the people who are cremated at the stations along the river—they call those stations *ghats*—are ordinary people who have lived impure lives. But there is a special category of persons who have lived pure lives—or at least it's supposed that they have. They include holy persons—Hindu sadhus and Buddhist monks. In addition, they include babies who died prematurely. These are pure beings and have the privilege of being buried in the holy River Ganges.

Adam: The privilege?

Barbara: Yes. As Mr. Shashank explained it, these special people are accorded the honor of being buried in the Ganges. Their bodies are wrapped in cloth, tied, and then anchored with heavy stones. When lowered into the river, the stones sink the bodies to the bottom of the river. In time, they decompose and become part of the holy Ganges.

Adam: Why do they do this?

Barbara: According to Hindu tradition, the Ganges is the embodiment of the life force itself. It's the source from which life begins, and it's the vehicle that transports the soul from one embodiment to another. The river is a hallowed medium for transmigration. That's what makes the Ganges so special. Since Hindu sadhus, Buddhist monks, and babies are taken to be morally uncontaminated, they are exempted from the usual method of cremation.

Nina: So it seems that sometimes the wrapping comes undone and the stones that are supposed to anchor the bodies somehow become disconnected. In those cases, babies sometimes float back to the surface. That's what we saw, isn't it, Barbara?

Barbara: Yes.

Nina: So we saw the result of an unsuccessful burial that was supposed to honor the pure baby.

Barbara: And all this was going on while Hindu sadhus and other meditators were congregated at the water's edge.

Relativism: A First Pass

Ronnie: That experience reminds me of the philosophy course we all took together at Canaday College. Remember those discussions we had about relativism?

Barbara: Yes, I sure do.

Ronnie: I've been thinking a lot about them since I arrived in India, where so much seems so different from what we're used to.

Adam: Why should our experience of the dead baby in the Ganges remind you of those discussions?

Ronnie: It seems to be a good example of relativism. It suggests that truth depends upon your point of view, your frame of reference.

Adam: Why do you say that?

Ronnie: Well, it's true for the Hindus that the Ganges is a hallowed medium. But for us, I guess, it's false that the Ganges is a hallowed medium.

Adam: Do you believe that the Ganges is a hallowed medium?

Ronnie: No, I don't. But that's not because I believe that claiming that it's hallowed is false, either. But that's me. I just don't think of rivers in terms of being hallowed or not. I don't understand how a river could or couldn't be a medium of transmigration. So I couldn't really say that it's false that the Ganges is a hallowed medium. But Adam, you believe the proposition is false. Don't you?

Adam: Yes. I believe that it's false that the Ganges is a hallowed medium. Maybe I'm wrong. For all I know, the Ganges really is a hallowed medium. My point is that it's either true or false that the Ganges is a hallowed medium. I may not know which, but there is a fact of the matter about it. You, Ronnie, seem to believe there's no fact of the matter. I guess you want to say that it's true for the Hindus that the Ganges is a hallowed medium and that it's false for us. I can't see how that could be possible.

Ronnie: You're right. I don't believe any absolute fact of the matter exists independent of any reference frame. Anyhow, even if there were such a fact of the matter, I'm not sure we could have access to it, so it wouldn't matter anyway, would it?

Adam: Do you believe you ought to adopt the Hindu view?

Ronnie: Not particularly. I just find it fascinating that they believe what they do. It's just so strange to me. That's all.

Adam: Those beliefs and practices are strange to me, too. But that doesn't yet make this an example of relativism. It's one thing to find that what they believe and do seems strange to us. It's another thing to say that what they believe is true for them and what they do is right for them.

Ronnie: Well, it's not only the strangeness of it. I also believe that for the Hindus, it really is true that the Ganges is a hallowed medium. For them it really is right that they bury their dead in the way that they do. If you see it from their point of view, it makes perfectly good sense.

Adam: Given their belief that the Ganges is hallowed, I see why they bury the people they believe are holy in the way they do.

Barbara: Of course, the burial practice initially looks strange to us because we don't believe what they believe. But, we can make sense of what they do, because we understand that when people die, their bodies should be treated with respect. Maybe their way of showing respect is very different from our way, but we do understand why they do what they do.

Ronnie: Still, from a secular Western reference frame—where we might take the Ganges to be a polluted and germ-infested body of water—the practice of submerging dead babies in the Ganges could amount to a disrespectful way of disposing of their bodies.

Adam: Yes, and it's worse than that. Sometimes the Indians urinate in the river. They dump dead buffalo in it. They do their laundry in it.

Nina: At the same time, though, the Ganges is a place where observant Hindus take ceremonial baths.

Ronnie: So, according to one reference frame, a submerged baby would have been dumped, and according to the other reference frame, it would have been honored.

Adam: I don't quite understand how you can explain that. How can they be both respectful and disrespectful of their dead at the same time?

Barbara: Well, as Mr. Shashank explained it, they believe that two Ganges Rivers actually exist. There's the pure medium, as pure as any could be, and there's the polluted body of water.

Adam: That's odd. How can you distinguish two rivers that comprise the Ganges? That makes no sense at all. Either the Ganges is hallowed or it's not.

Barbara: I suppose what Mr. Shashank meant was that, while all that debris is in the water, the Ganges—in its essence, inherently, intrinsically—is pure. We can distinguish the pure Ganges from the polluted water. We can distinguish the hallowed from the defiled. In its pure form, the Ganges is hallowed.

Adam: So what does that tell us about relativism? Ronnie, don't get me wrong. I'm fascinated by how different people come to believe what they believe, and how certain practices emerge from that. But I'm also interested in what is true or right. So when you tell me that a given belief can be true for one group of people and false for another group—above and beyond the fact that they happen to believe something or behave in some particular way—then I'm puzzled.

Ronnie: I see why you're puzzled. But I just don't see how you could believe that it's true or not true that the Ganges is a hallowed medium independent of any reference frame—theirs or any other. As Mr. Shashank explained it, from the Hindu point of view, the Ganges is a hallowed medium for transmigration and reincarnation. It is so for them. It is not so for us.

Nina: So, Ronnie, you're saying that there are no givens. There are only takens. There are no facts without their being taken one way or another, without their being taken as something or other.

Ronnie: Precisely.

Nina: You know, Ronnie, while I follow your thought about there being only takens and no givens, I'm not so sure about your talk about us and them. While I've been at the ashram for a few years now, sometimes I think myself more as one of them. But that's not quite right either. I'm not even sure there is an "us" or "them."

Adam: Can you give us another sort of example of relativism, Ronnie?

Further Examples of Relativism

Ronnie: Sure. We know that the earth rotates around the sun. But we know it only if we take the sun as fixed. Yet there's no fact of the matter as to whether we should take the sun as fixed. We could as well take the earth as fixed. If we take the sun as fixed, the earth revolves around the sun. If we take the earth as fixed, the sun revolves around the earth. That's a matter of convention. It's a matter of our purposes and interests.

Adam: I don't get it.

Ronnie: If you take the sun as fixed, it's true that the earth travels around the sun. If you take the earth as fixed, it's true that the sun travels around the earth. But there's nothing that requires you to take one or the other as fixed. Yet if you do take the sun as fixed, it's wrong to deny that the earth travels around it. If you take the earth as fixed, it's wrong to deny that the sun travels around it.

Adam: I suppose next you're going to tell us that, if we take an even further point as fixed, both the earth and the sun would rotate relative to that point.

Ronnie: Exactly. Whichever point you take as fixed, it's not absolutely given. Even if you hold fixed such a distant star as Alpha Centauri in the constellation of Centaurus—which is about 4.37 light years away—even then, taking that as fixed is a matter of convention. It's not absolute.

Barbara: So, in some sense—other than Adam's absolute sense—there is a fact, but only as constructed within the terms of a reference frame. Once you have indicated your reference frame, there are facts within it. Taking the sun as fixed, it is true that the earth revolves around the sun. Taking Alpha Centauri as fixed, it is true that both the sun and the earth rotate around it. But there's no fact of the matter, independent of all reference frames, as to what revolves around what.

Ronnie: That's exactly right.

Barbara: You know, Ronnie, your examples about the rotations of the moon, the earth, and Alpha Centauri remind me of a joke I once heard.

Ronnie: Oh yes? Tell us.

Barbara: OK. A woman calls her husband on his cell phone while he's driving on the Los Angeles freeway. She's worried about him. She had just heard a news flash on the radio that there's a car on the freeway that's going in the wrong direction. It's causing mayhem. So she calls him to warn him that he had better be careful.

Ronnie: So then what happens?

Barbara: Well, he says to his wife, "Yes, I know. I just heard about it on the radio too. It's true. I can see the confusion all around me, and you know what? It's not just that one car either. There are hundreds of cars that are coming at me in the wrong direction!"

Ronnie: That's really funny. But, you know, it does illustrate my point.

Adam: What's that?

Ronnie: It shows that going in the right or wrong direction is not a matter of an absolute fact. They are relative to a reference frame. The truth about the right or wrong direction is a matter of convention. In this way, we can talk about truth or rightness, but only within the context of some reference frame. Given our shared purposes and interests—like keeping from being hit by other cars—we can mutually decide which reference frames are better than others. But there's no fact of the matter as such.

Adam: But we need some grounds—some absolute grounds—to settle which reference frame ultimately is the right one. Ronnie, you seem to believe that discussions about particular purposes and interests will be enough. But I just don't believe that appealing to particular purposes and interests allows you to rank reference frames. Most people have conflicting agendas. They have different purposes and interests. I wouldn't count on discussions about purposes and interests to settle which reference frames are better than others.

Ronnie: But you could have critical discussions about purposes and interests. It's just that they don't have to be grounded in absolute standards, that is, standards independent of any reference frames. Those judgments don't have to be arbitrary. We can say that one frame is preferable to another without assuming that there are absolutist standards. One frame would be better than another if the first helps us to negotiate ourselves in situations—like driving our cars. Which frame is better than another depends upon the purposes or interests.

Adam: OK. So let's shift the example a bit. Let's talk about cars themselves. Cars exist. They exist independent of any frames.

Ronnie: Yes, they exist. But they exist as cars—as ordinary middle-sized objects that we can see and feel. As cars, they can collide with, make dents in, or even destroy other cars. But notice this. Cars as collections of subatomic particles don't collide with other cars.

Adam: That's crazy. When a car hits you—and I sure hope it doesn't— you tell me whether it's just a matter of a reference frame.

Ronnie: It *is* a matter of a reference frame. It's not *just* a matter of a reference frame.

Adam: It's a fact, independent of reference frames, that a car can hit another car or, sadly, a human being. End of story.

Ronnie: That's not the end of the story. It's only an abbreviated story. The longer story is that it's true that a car is able to hit another car or hit a human being. It's true at one level of description, and that level is the level of middle-sized objects. But if you magnify a bit of a car or a person many times over, you'd see subatomic phenomena in empty space. At that level of description, cars and persons no longer appear. There are no cars or persons at a subatomic level of description.

Adam: So, are you saying that cars and persons don't exist? That would be foolish.

Ronnie: No. I'm saying there really are cars and persons, and there really are subatomic phenomena. But each exists at a particular level of description. And no one level of description is the only one right level. Not everything that is true about cars is true about subatomic phenomena, and vice versa. There is no inherent fact of the matter—no fact independent of a reference frame.

Adam: Ronnie, I guess you're next going to tell me that the existence of this table that supports my cup of tea—as a table—depends upon some reference frame.

Ronnie: Yes, that's exactly right. There really is a table—but only at one level of description, within the context of one particular reference frame.

Adam: And what reference frame is that?

Ronnie: It's the reference frame of middle-sized objects.

Adam: Come on, Ronnie. Here's the table and here's my cup that's sitting on it, period. That's that. End of story.

Ronnie: No. Why do you keep wanting to cut the story short? We're always in the middle of the story. At a subatomic level, there are no tables and no cups.

Adam: OK. But there must be an ultimate level of description, one that describes the most fundamental constituents of ultimate reality. Surely there must be a limit. Maybe the end of the story is composed of electrons or even smaller subatomic phenomena in empty space. Maybe it's composed of some undifferentiated unity or some unformed stuff. But there's got to be some ultimate reality that doesn't depend upon some reference frame or other.

Ronnie: No, I don't believe that there is a most basic, most fundamental stuff, or level, of description. I believe it's infinitely analyzable. There's no end to it.

Adam: So you don't believe that there's a final deep ultimate reality at all?

Ronnie: I believe there's a reality, but always understood within some reference frame. I believe no deepest final reality independent of any reference frame exists.

A Definition of Relativism

Nina: Ronnie, I guess I have a general idea about what you're driving at by relativism. But maybe it's time to define it a bit more precisely.

Adam: Yes. Good idea.

Ronnie: OK. Let me take a stab at it. *Relativism claims that truth, goodness, or beauty is relative to a reference frame, and no absolute, overarching standards to adjudicate between competing reference frames exist.* How's that for a general definition of relativism?

Barbara: Ronnie, I guess your definition—which really has two parts—captures what you've been saying about the baby in the Ganges, the rotation of the earth around the sun, the solar system, the car on the freeway, this table, and the tea cup.

Adam: OK. So let's go with your definition for now.

Nina: I take it, Ronnie, that you believe that the opposite of relativism is absolutism, right?

Ronnie: Yes. *Absolutism asserts that truth, goodness, or beauty is not relative to a reference frame, and absolutist standards to adjudicate between reference frames do exist.*

Nina: So if we think of relativism as negating the absolutist claim—including the second part that says that absolutist standards for adjudicating between reference frames exist—we'll need to ask, "What are absolutist standards?"

Ronnie: Right. But before we do that, though, maybe we should think a bit about a couple of other views that are sometimes confused with relativism.

Adam: What do you have in mind, Ronnie?

What Relativism Is Not

Ronnie: Well, take the idea of diversity. I mean, Hindus believe that the Ganges is a hallowed medium, and we don't. They consign their holy people to it. We don't. As you said, Adam, just because our beliefs and practices are different doesn't automatically amount to relativism. We shouldn't confuse relativism with the simple observation that different people have different beliefs or pursue different practices. The fact that different people believe different things and behave in different ways doesn't make you a relativist. Diversity doesn't automatically amount to relativism.

Adam: I'm glad we agree about that.

Ronnie: Still, relativism at least starts from the observation of diversity. If no diversity existed, we would have no temptation to go on to say that truth is relative to different reference frames. The same goes for goodness and beauty.

Adam: Of course, different people hold different views about things and pursue different practices. But some of those beliefs just are true or false, and some of those practices are right or wrong, period. They correspond to the facts of the matter. They accord with frame-independent facts.

Barbara: Be that as it may, at least we should be able to agree that the fact of diversity—that different peoples embrace different beliefs and practices—is not tantamount to the claim of relativism. That's not yet relativism. Are we agreed about that?

Ronnie: Yes, I think so. What about you, Nina?

Nina: I'm with you on that. Now Ronnie, what else should we not confuse with relativism?

Ronnie: Take fallibilism. Fallibilism doesn't amount to relativism either.

Barbara: What's fallibilism?

Ronnie: Fallibilism is the idea that, no matter what we believe, we could always be wrong. We can't believe anything with complete certainty because, after all, we are human.

Adam: Correct. An absolutist could also be a fallibilist. Some people might believe that absolutism commits you to the idea that you can't be wrong, that what you know, you know with certainty. That's a mistaken understanding of absolutism though. All absolutism claims is that truth—or goodness or beauty for that matter—is independent of any reference frame. It doesn't say that you or I actually know the truth at any given time.

Ronnie: So the possibility that you might be wrong about what you believe is not something that is unique to either relativism or absolutism.

Barbara: Surely, both the absolutist and the relativist can agree about that. Both of them allow that, while there may or may not be a fact of the matter independent of reference frames, whatever you believe at any given time, you could be wrong.

Nina: Right. An absolutist could understand the idea of a false belief in terms of a mismatch between a statement and a frame-independent fact of the matter. And a relativist could understand the idea of a false belief in terms of a mismatch between a statement and facts as constructed within a reference frame. Either way, neither relativism nor absolutism has a special claim on fallibilism.

Barbara: OK. So, fallibilism is not a uniquely defining feature of either relativism or absolutism. Fallibilism is compatible with both of them. You could be a fallibilist and either a relativist or an absolutist. Got it.

Reference Frames

Nina: So, now that we're clearer about what relativism isn't, Ronnie, let's go back to your definition. You've partly defined relativism as claiming that truth, goodness, or beauty is relative to a reference frame. You keep using the idea of a reference frame. But I'm not sure what constitutes a reference frame.

Adam: Yes, I'm puzzled about that too.

Ronnie: Well, consider the heliocentric and geocentric pictures of the solar system. Does the earth travel around the sun, or does the sun travel around the earth? There's no fact of the matter about it. But one reference frame takes one thing as a given, and another reference frame takes something else as a given. I'd say that a reference frame is a kind of system or point of view that takes things in a particular way. It provides the terms for understanding something as the thing it is.

Adam: Could I say that my reference frame is my present unique situation, call it my "me-here-now?"

Ronnie: What do you mean?

Adam: I mean, could I designate my present unique situation as my reference frame?

Ronnie: If you do that, if you say that truth is relative to your unique situation, then whatever you say must be true. Your saying so would make it so. Is that what you're driving at?

Adam: Yes. I know that it's a pretty extreme case. Your me-here-now would be your reference frame or point of view. It would contrast with my me-here-now. But that would lead to a breakdown of communication.

Barbara: If what many people believe were true because they believe it, you'd have many people talking past each other. Clearly that won't do.

Adam: I'm relieved that we agree about that. Let's see what happens if we consider a reference frame that's not a unique me-here-now reference frame.

Ronnie: Fine. So let's consider the claim that truth is relative to a culture, or to a religion. You could say that, for Hindus, it's true that the Ganges is a hallowed medium. For Western secularists, it's not true.

Adam: But here again, we could get the possibility of the same communication breakdown that we get with the me-here-now's. It's just that here, we have the breakdown between groups rather than between individuals' subjective reference frames.

Nina: You know, Ronnie, there's something else that's odd about the idea of a reference frame. I'm wondering if it's so easy to identify reference frames to start with.

Ronnie: What do you mean, Nina?

Nina: Well, the idea of a reference frame makes sense only if you can differentiate one frame from another, as numerically distinct. If you can't do that, then the idea of diversity of reference frames wouldn't get off the ground in the first place. Moreover, the relativist depends upon the idea of diversity of reference frames.

Barbara: Can you give an example?

Nina: Sure. Some anthropologists have suggested that different languages reflect different ways of understanding the world. For example, the Hopi language of North American Indians is supposed to be structured in such a way that it allows you to describe things only in terms of dynamic processes rather than static products, verbs rather than nouns, actions rather than fixed states. So, if in English, I would say, "Barbara is sitting," in Hopi, the Indian would say something like, "Sitting is going on in a Barbara-like fashion." In other words, you, Barbara, would be described in adverbial terms.

Barbara: OK. What does that have to do with the idea of a reference frame?

Nina: Well, if one language is a dynamic process-centered language, and another language is a static product-centered language, and if they are not mutually translatable, you'd have two distinct reference frames. That would be fine for the relativist who needs a diversity of reference frames. But here's the rub. If the two languages were translatable, then they wouldn't count as two distinct languages at all. In fact, I just told a story to show how they might be related and that suggests that they are translatable.

Barbara: So, to have two languages, you'd need for them to be untranslatable?

Nina: Right. But the problem with that is, if they really are untranslatable, then neither the English speaker nor the Hopi—nor, for that matter, I—could tell if there were a second language at all. We could not understand the other language to tell!

Barbara: Oh, so then, the possibility that there really is a diversity of languages would be called into question. Is that it?

Nina: That's it. Without that diversity of reference frames, you couldn't distinguish between reference frames. The very idea of a reference frame would be questionable. Actually, the problem here is generalizable. If any two would-be reference frames really were translatable, then there would be no pairs of reference frames. In addition, if there were no two reference frames to distinguish one from another, the idea of a single reference frame would have no content.

Barbara: So how would that affect the idea of relativism?

Nina: If you define relativism in terms of the idea of a reference frame, and that idea has no content, then the idea of relativism would have no content. That's the problem.

Ronnie: Nina, you're assuming that non-translatability is necessary to distinguish between two reference frames.

Nina: Yes.

Ronnie: What if non-translatability isn't a necessary condition to distinguish between them?

Nina: What do you mean, Ronnie?

Ronnie: Couldn't a person from one reference frame understand someone from another reference frame, even if the second reference frame wasn't translatable into the first? Actually, bilingual people do that all the time. When bilingual persons understand utterances of different languages, you don't believe they really have to translate between the languages, do you? You don't believe that bilingual Hopi and English speakers are actually translating between Hopi and English when they speak or hear Hopi or English, do you? Non-translatability need not be a problem for there to be different reference frames. Yet they can understand each other. Moreover, they can note that important differences exist between their languages, their reference frames. I think the idea of a reference frame remains intact.

Nina: I guess you could be right about that.

Ronnie: One more thing. Even if some would-be reference frames turned out not to be numerically distinct from one another, that wouldn't mean that all would-be reference frames are not distinct from one another. All relativists need, to make their case, is for some pairs of reference frames to exist, and, of course, for no absolutist standards to adjudicate between them to exist.

Nina: I guess you're right about that too.

Ronnie: We didn't have any problem distinguishing between the heliocentric and geocentric pictures of the solar system, did we? We didn't have any problem distinguishing between a Hindu reference frame of the Ganges and a secular Western reference frame of the Ganges, did we?

Barbara: No we didn't.

Adam: Ronnie, I'm not so easily convinced. I remain suspicious about your idea of a reference frame.

Ronnie: Why so?

Adam: Let's go back to the case of the Ganges River. You're saying that the Hindu view, for example, amounts to one reference frame, and the secular Western view amounts to another. Right?

Ronnie: Yes, and there's no absolute fact of the matter to adjudicate between those reference frames.

Reference Frames and Beliefs

Adam: Well, I don't know what you're building into this phrase, "reference frame." I don't understand why you want to anoint Hindu beliefs with the shroud of a so-called reference frame. It sounds obscure to me.

Ronnie: What do you mean?

Adam: Why not simply say that the Hindus, on the one hand, share particular beliefs about the hallowedness of the Ganges, for example, and acknowledge as well, that we don't share those beliefs. Then we could go on to consider whether those beliefs are true or false and then decide about that?

Barbara: Oh. I see. You would rather talk about beliefs rather than reference frames.

Adam: Yes. I think that talk about reference frames is a way of keeping us from critically assessing beliefs.

Barbara: Why should that be?

Adam: Well, when you cast beliefs within so-called reference frames, you seem to shield them from questions about whether they are true or false, right or wrong. I want to be able to ask those kinds of questions. Of course, I can ask those kinds of questions if all you mean by the Hindu's reference frame, for example, is that they believe that the Ganges is a hallowed medium for transmigration and reincarnation. But you seem to believe that the idea of a reference is more than that, don't you?

Ronnie: Yes. A reference frame provides a point of view, a perspective, in terms of which we orient ourselves as to what we take to exist. Our individual beliefs are structured in the terms that reference frames provide. How we distinguish between, and categorize, objects of the world depends upon reference frames. Without some reference frame, we couldn't even make individual beliefs intelligible to ourselves or to anyone else. Without reference frames, we would have no way to organize our perceptions or thoughts, no way to communicate our ideas, no way to grasp values, or evaluate behavior. Without reference frames, we'd be without orientation.

Barbara: All right. Then don't you think we should be able to criticize and evaluate reference frames? How would that be possible?

Ronnie: Talk of reference frames doesn't disallow criticism. Sometimes, we don't know what to say about the rightness of one reference frame or another. But other times, we can say such things as that, for certain purposes, it's more useful to think of the earth as fixed. Or, for other purposes, it's more useful to think of the sun as fixed. Still at other times, it's more useful to think of other celestial bodies as fixed. That may not be what you have in mind when you ask about criticism, but it's those sorts of considerations of purposes and interests that relativists rely on in critical discussions.

Adjudication and Sameness

Nina: Maybe there's another snag with relativism. Ronnie, the second part of your definition mentions adjudication; that is, ranking between competing reference frames. But for reference frames to really compete with each other—rather than talking past each other—they would have to be talking about the same thing. If they don't talk about the same thing, then they can't compete.

Ronnie: What are you getting at, Nina?

Nina: Well, when we talk about the Ganges, are we talking about the same thing as what the Hindu is talking about? If we focus on the debris in the Ganges—including the remains of buffalo and other such things—and the Hindu focuses on the inner meaning of the Ganges, are we talking about different things or the same thing, the same river Ganges? If we're talking about different things, we'd be talking past each other. If the reference frames don't address the same thing, they can't really compete with each other, can they?

Ronnie: So?

Adam: So, for people who embrace different reference frames to compete, they would need to address a single fact of the matter, independent of any reference frame.

Ronnie: Yes. I agree that, for people who embrace different reference frames to agree or disagree, they would have to be talking about the same thing. But they could come to agree that what they are talking about is the same thing—or not, for that matter—by comparing the meanings of their terms. Different people could have different views about polygamy, for instance, in accord with their respective reference frames, but they could agree that they are talking about the same thing, namely, a marriage arrangement. That would also be frame-relative. I don't see why people of different reference frames couldn't come to agree that they are talking about the same thing.

Adam: But, they could come to an agreement about such commonality and still be wrong. They need to be able to make such judgments based on their access to facts of the matter independent of such agreements.

Ronnie: But we never do have access to such frame-independent facts of the matter.

Nina: You know, this question of sameness of what different reference frames are talking about reminds me of conversations I had with my Hindu Swamiji, and with my friend Geshe Samten, who is a Tibetan Buddhist monk in Sarnath.

Barbara: Tell us.

Nina: Well, I asked Swamiji whether, when he talks about the general nature of reality, he is talking about the same thing as what Buddhists are talking about when they discuss reality.

Barbara: What did he say?

Nina: He said yes, the Hindu and the Buddhist are talking about the same thing, but the Buddhist is wrong.

Barbara: What did your Buddhist friend Geshe Samten say?

Nina: When I asked Geshe Samten whether the Buddhist and the Hindu are talking about the same thing, he said, no, they are not talking about the same thing.

Adam: So, you're saying that they disagree about whether they disagree with each other?

Nina: Precisely. If they are not talking about the same thing, they can't disagree.

Ronnie: That's an intriguing case. They are disagreeing about whether they are disagreeing.

Adam: Let me get this straight. Just because they are disagreeing about whether they are disagreeing, couldn't one of them just be wrong? Or for that matter, couldn't both of them be wrong? I mean there must be a fact of the matter, no matter what each of them believes.

Ronnie: In such cases, it's impossible to know.

Adam: In such cases? What cases do you mean? What's so special about this case?

Nina: Swamiji says that all is One—that when we distinguish, say, between individuals such as you and me, or between this table and this cup, we are introducing distinctions at a conventional, or, as he says, at a relative human level. But really, what he calls absolute is the all-pervasive One, the inherent One. That's all that there really is.

Adam: What does Geshe Samten say?

Nina: He agrees that all distinctions are relative or conventional. But beyond distinctions—at the most fundamental level—he believes that all things are empty of inherent existence, including all individuals and Oneness.

Adam: So, Nina, how does this case bear on the question of the commonality of a subject between people of different reference frames?

Nina: Well, it strikes me that even though two people may appear to have a disagreement about what they are talking about—in this case about the ultimate nature of reality—they can't really make a judgment about an assumed commonality of a subject if they also hold, as Swamiji and Samten do, that all talk is constrained by the limits of language. They both assume you can't get at the ultimate nature of reality by using language. This would be a case in which two persons, operating from within different reference frames, can't really come to an agreement about whether they are talking about the same thing. So they couldn't really say whether they are agreeing or disagreeing. They both believe that what they address themselves to is beyond language.

Adam: But still, why can't one or both of them be wrong? Why can't one of their views just not correspond with the facts of the matter?

Nina: More to the point, the question should be, "Why can't they come to agree that they are talking about the same thing?" I guess the answer has to be that they agree that what they are talking about can't be talked about. While Swamiji does, in a general way, talk about the ultimate nature of reality in terms of Atman or Oneness, and, while Geshe Samten also in a general way does talk about the ultimate nature of reality in terms of the negation of Atman, or Anatman, or Emptiness, they both agree that, insofar as they talk at all, they falsify the ultimate nature of reality. So under those conditions, they can't really say whether they are talking about the same thing or not. That's my point.

Ronnie: I guess that's why they can't appeal to some frame-independent fact of the matter as to whether their beliefs about the ultimate nature of reality are true or false.

Adam: I agree. There's something peculiar about this sort of case. They both hold that what ultimately exists can't be captured in any language. According to them, what exists is ultimately ineffable.

Nina: I guess I'm saying that Swamiji was wrong to say that they were talking about the same thing, and Geshe Samten was wrong to say that they weren't talking about the same thing. To be correct, they both should have answered that neither of them could say!

Adam: Well, whatever they should have said, there must be a fact of the matter as to whether what ultimately exists is expressible in language. Maybe they are both wrong to believe that no language can capture the ultimate nature of reality.

Facts of the Matter

Barbara: Adam, you keep using this phrase, "fact of the matter." What do you mean by that?

Adam: By a fact of the matter, I mean facts that exist independent of any reference frame. Ultimately, a reality, as such, must exist independent of all reference frames. I'm disturbed by the idea of a world without facts of the matter.

Ronnie: As I understand you, Adam, facts of the matter are different from what I think of as facts. I think of facts as constructed within a reference frame. So, then, going back to our example of the baby in the Ganges, no frame-independent fact of the matter exists as to whether the Hindu or the Western secularist is right. That's why I say that is a case of relativism.

Adam: But Ronnie, even if you're right to say that we can't understand the world without some reference frame, or if you're right that we can't say anything at all without some language or other, it doesn't follow that no world independent of reference frames exists. Even if we can't discover them, regardless of what anybody believes, there must be facts of the matter. I don't see how you can say no facts of the matter exist.

Ronnie: But I don't say there are no facts of the matter. I say no one could *know* whether facts of the matter exist. I say only that *if* facts of the matter exist, independent of our knowledge about them, of what use would they be?

Adam: What use would they be? What kind of question is that?

Ronnie: I mean that anything you do say obviously is said, and anything that is said can be said only as filtered through some reference frame. So, I can't make out what it could be that would be independent of some reference frame.

Barbara: Even if there were frame-independent facts of the matter, without access to them, they wouldn't help us to adjudicate anything.

Ronnie: Also, whatever it is that you think you identify as facts of the matter, all you would be doing would be postulating. When you do that, all you are doing is assigning a privileged starting point in an inquiry, assuming a presupposition as basic to an inquiry. When you do that, though, you haven't identified a frame-independent fact of the matter.

Adam: But your view, Ronnie, doesn't allow you to say that any beliefs are just wrong. That's a problem for me. You couldn't say that a belief doesn't accord with the facts. How could you say any beliefs can be wrong? I just don't see it.

Ronnie: You want to know how I can account for wrongness if I don't have available to me frame-independent facts of the matter.

Adam: Exactly!

Ronnie: I say that someone is wrong if one's belief doesn't accord with other beliefs that person holds. For example, one is wrong to believe that the earth is flat if, at the same time, that person finds the photographs of the earth shot at a great distance from it to be convincing; or if, despite one's belief that the earth is flat, that person believes the testimony of experts to the contrary.

Adam: Wait a minute. You agree that this person is wrong to believe that the earth is flat, right?

Ronnie: Yes.

Adam: In addition, you say that this person is wrong because the belief does not accord with his or her other beliefs?

Ronnie: Yes. That person is wrong in holding that belief if it is inconsistent with other beliefs the person holds, or inconsistent with others' beliefs whom the person regards as experts.

Adam: But those other beliefs, against which people check their belief about the flatness of the earth, may not themselves reflect frame-independent facts of the matter.

Ronnie: Right.

Adam: I don't get it. If there are no frame-independent facts of the matter, how can anyone be convinced that the belief is wrong? Why should one give any credence to those other beliefs with which the first belief is supposed to cohere? How do those other beliefs get any traction? We need the idea of a frame-independent world to make sense of the idea of right or wrong.

Ronnie: But to assume that a frame-independent world of facts of the matter exists, as such, is superfluous. It does no work for us within the practice of our inquiries. It may feel reassuring to believe that there is something out there, but it doesn't actually help us to determine which beliefs are right or wrong. Whether explicit or not, any and all claims about what exists assume that they are relative to some reference frame. It's relative all the way down.

Adam: Ronnie, even if that were true about anything we would wish to say, that needn't be the case for what actually exists. What exists is not determined by what we can or can't say about what exists.

Ronnie: You distinguish between what we can say and what exists. But notice that your distinction between what we can say and what exists is something that you've said—said, that is, from within a reference frame. By drawing that distinction, you haven't encountered what exists independent of what you say. I'd think that you would have to remain silent about what you think is frame-independent.

Adam: But most of the time we do have access to frame-independent facts of the matter. Just look at the Ganges, touch this table, taste your tea, hear the bustle of human activity from the road below.

Ronnie: I hardly think those are examples of frame-independent facts of the matter. It's not clear what it is that I'm supposed to be looking at when you invite me to look at the Ganges. Is it a hallowed medium I'm looking at? A body of water made up of hydrogen and oxygen? When you ask me to touch this table, how do I distinguish between this table and that one? How do I distinguish between tea and coffee? Don't I need to judge whether the bustle you mention is caused by something in the road below in contrast to the sound from the overhead fan?

Adam: Even if I grant that there are frame-dependent inferences or interpretations in those cases—and I'm not at all sure I should—there must still be something there—some absolute stuff before us, stuff out of which the Ganges or this table or teacup or, for that matter, physical human beings are made.

An Undifferentiated Reality

Nina: But Adam, this absolute stuff that you mention—this stuff that precedes our identifying any particular thing to be the thing that we take it to be—would have to be undifferentiated. At the same time, keeping in mind our definition of relativism that excludes absolutist standards for adjudication between reference frames, you would need differentiated facts of the matter to adjudicate between reference frames. Even if we had access to it, frame-independent undifferentiated stuff couldn't provide the standards necessary for adjudication.

Ronnie: I don't understand this talk about differentiated and undifferentiated stuff. I understand what it would be like not to know or not to have access to facts of the matter. But what do you mean when you say stuff might be undifferentiated?

Nina: Try this. By undifferentiated stuff I mean something that has no individuated parts. Not only could you not count its parts, but you couldn't even say that the stuff is one thing or another. But, it was Adam who suggested the idea of absolute undifferentiated stuff.

Adam: Yes. I can imagine that behind all individuated things—before they were individuated—there must have been undifferentiated stuff out of which the individual objects of the world were made.

Ronnie: But, as Nina says, even if a frame-independent undifferentiated reality exists, it couldn't help you to adjudicate anything. You couldn't get help for adjudicating between reference frames by appealing to not-yet differentiated stuff. To say that there exists an undifferentiated reality won't help you to adjudicate between the heliocentric or the geocentric system of the solar system, for example.

Adam: So to adjudicate you'd have to assume that there are differentiated objects to appeal to.

Nina: Right.

Barbara: But even if undifferentiated stuff existed, how could you have access to it?

Nina: I guess that would require special powers, a special kind of intuition, a special sensibility, maybe revelation. But I doubt that Ronnie could make sense of that special sensibility.

Ronnie: I agree with you on that, Nina. I can't make sense of the kind of intuition or revelation that that would require.

Barbara: So, this is where we've come, right? Adam would need differentiated frame-independent objects to adjudicate between reference frames. But Ronnie believes that we have no access to such differentiated frame-independent objects. And even if we had access to an underlying undifferentiated stuff—which would be unlikely—there's the question of its ability to help us adjudicate anything at all.

Nina: That pretty well sums it up.

Barbara: Right. To adjudicate, you need differentiated resources. And the not-yet differentiated stuff is just that—not-yet-differentiated.

Nina: Precisely. But remember, the relativist is only denying that absolutist frame-independent ways of adjudicating between reference frames exist. So, Ronnie could still allow that there could be this not-yet-differentiated stuff. It just couldn't adjudicate between reference frames.

Barbara: So you could deny that there are frame-independent ways of adjudicating between reference frames, and at the same time hold that this undifferentiated frame-independent stuff exists. Going back to what Nina said about Hinduism, you could embrace the absolute undifferentiated Atma, Oneness, and still be relativist according to the definition of relativism.

Nina: Bingo! Even if this not-yet-differentiated stuff were frame-independent, you couldn't say, for example, that the statement, "This cup is on this table" is true if it corresponds to the not-yet-differentiated stuff. You couldn't say that the statement, "The shortest distance between two points is a straight line in Euclidean geometry" is true if it corresponds to the not-yet-differentiated stuff. It's not clear how a statement can correspond to a frame-independent undifferentiated stuff.

Ronnie: I see that.

Nina: So, Ronnie, even if there were an undifferentiated reality that hovers behind reference frames, it wouldn't make any difference as it regards your relativism.

Ronnie: Still, I could imagine someone calling the undifferentiated reality the Absolute. If the undifferentiated reality could count as an absolute, my definition might allow for some kind of absolutism. That wouldn't be a good thing for me.

Nina: But somebody's calling the undifferentiated reality a kind of absolute may not be as damaging as you might at first think, Ronnie. If I recall correctly, your definition says that relativism claims that truth, goodness, or beauty is relative to a reference frame, and no absolute standards to adjudicate between competing reference frames exist. Your definition concerns the non-existence of absolute standards to adjudicate between reference frames. A presumed undifferentiated reality couldn't adjudicate anything— even if it still existed, even absolutely. I don't see that you have to exclude everything that might be called absolute to preserve your definition of relativism. All your definition needs is to exclude absolute standards to adjudicate between references frames—and it does that.

Ronnie: Thanks, Nina. I can see that it really doesn't matter whether I don't deny an absolute undifferentiated reality. All I really need to care about is the question of adjudication, and the undifferentiated reality couldn't do any adjudicating in any case.

Barbara: But Nina, even if you're right to help save Ronnie's definition of relativism—let me call it a functional definition—there might still be a point to calling the undifferentiated reality a kind of absolute. Surely it would be frame-independent. Sometimes relativism is taken to deny absolutism—all absolutisms—including the absolutism of an undifferentiated unity. But according to your definition of relativism, Ronnie, one could be a kind of relativist, a functional relativist, and at the same time you could be a kind of absolutist; let me call it a transcendental absolutist. Actually I like that kind of reconciliation.

Nina: What do you think, Adam?

Adam: Well, I think the question of an undifferentiated reality is a red herring. I can't make sense of the idea of an undifferentiated reality at all. I think it's incoherent. So as far as I'm concerned, Ronnie's definition of relativism is fine. I believe absolutism stands or falls on whether absolutist standards can adjudicate between reference frames. Unlike Ronnie, I believe that they can. There are frame-independent facts of the matter, and most often, we have access to them.

Ronnie: I guess Adam and I share a functionalist attitude. If it couldn't do any adjudicatory work, why bother with the concept of an undifferentiated reality? Why burden ourselves with negating the idea of an undifferentiated reality? Why not remain agnostic on the point? I'd rather keep my metaphysics as light as possible.

The World and Its Objects

Adam: I have a different view about the world. The world is already composed of differentiated frame-independent objects to begin with. So I don't even have to try to make sense of this mysterious idea of a not-yet-differentiated reality. And you know what? We do have access to differentiated objects of the world. Just look around you. You see the trees and the water, don't you? The statement, "Trees exist" is true because trees do exist irrespective of reference frames. These are frame-independent objects that make up the world—that's that. Generally speaking, we have access to such objects. I believe that the world is composed of distinct, countable, differentiated objects. But Ronnie, you keep talking about the problem of access to the way the world is, because we can only know what has been filtered via reference frames.

Ronnie: Yes.

Adam: Well, even if you're right about that—and I don't say that you are—there might be a way to argue for the absolutist view that gets around the question of access.

Ronnie: What's that?

Adam: Consider a hypothetical version of facts of the matter, an "as if" version.

Ronnie: What would that look like?

Adam: Even if we can't have access to the way the world is—and I don't say we can't—this modified version would hold that it would be useful to assume—hypothetically—that we could have such access.

Ronnie: How would that affect our conduct of inquiry?

Adam: It would give us hope. We could at least assume that our best efforts would be in the service of getting the story right, to accord with the way the world is. It would motivate us to get at the truth even if we could not know that we had come upon it when we had.

Ronnie: I understand why you say that, Adam. But I don't see why your "as if" version would help in our inquiry. It wouldn't help to determine if we're getting closer to the truth.

Nina: Also, Adam, your "as if" version wouldn't provide what your original version of facts of the matter might promise—that is, to adjudicate between reference frames. An "as if" version of facts of the matter couldn't provide a way for us to do that.

Frame-Independence and Progress

Adam: I suppose you're right about that, Nina. But still, the idea of a frame-independent world would be central to our understanding of progress. You can't just let it go.

Barbara: Why not?

Adam: Because without it, we couldn't make sense of the idea of progress in increasing or improving our knowledge of the world. We progress only insofar as what we say about the world gets truer of it. We progress insofar as our knowledge approximates or corresponds with the world. If you drop the idea of the world, you couldn't make sense of the idea of progress of knowledge.

Barbara: But if we can't know that it does so, does it really matter?

Adam: Yes, even so. Without it, we couldn't make sense of the idea of progress in the history of science, for example.

Barbara: Why couldn't we just say that our knowledge grows to the extent that it becomes more coherent or more useful? That's progress enough, isn't it?

Adam: That might be progress. But it's not the kind of progress I'm after.

Barbara: Well, maybe you can't have the kind of progress you're after. The history of science is progressive only in this modest sense. It helps to make our concepts coherent and to control our environment. But that doesn't commit us to saying that there is a frame-independent world that we know, that our knowledge correctly approximates that world. If we have no access to the frame-independent world, what's the point of invoking that frame-independent world?

Adam: But Barbara, I'm still worried that even if you were to reject the idea of facts of the matter as being of no use, surely you don't want to say that all reference frames could be equally admissible. You can't allow just any reference frame.

Ronnie: You're right about that, Adam. Which reference frames are relevant depends upon the circumstances, upon our purposes and interests.

Adam: So you think that there are no general criteria that will allow you to say that one reference frame is better than another?

Ronnie: No, I don't think so.

Adam: That sounds pretty arbitrary to me.

Ronnie: I don't know why you say that. Just because there are no general rules for picking out which, of a number of possible reference frames, one should choose, that doesn't mean that choosing one over another in a particular situation is arbitrary. My regarding this thing as a table or as a collection of electrons depends upon my purposes and interests. That doesn't make the choice arbitrary.

Adam: But ultimately, there must be a reality—a fact of the matter—independent of all reference frames. Ultimately, it must be that a God's eye point of view exists.

God's Eye Point of View

Ronnie: I've always found the idea of a God's eye point of view kind of odd. Even if God's eye point of view were the most comprehensive point of view, it would still be a point of view. It would be an imperial point of view, or an all-inclusive reference frame—one that includes all other reference frames. It would be the reference frame of all reference frames. But even then, such an imperial reference frame would still be a reference frame.

Nina: The idea of an imperial reference frame is interesting, Ronnie. If there were an imperial reference frame of all reference frames, then there could be no second reference frame.

Ronnie: So?

Nina: That means that the question of adjudicating between more than one reference frames would not even arise. You need two or more reference frames for the question to arise. If there's only one imperial reference frame, you wouldn't even need to search for anything that would adjudicate at all. So, Ronnie, even if you allowed the idea of an imperial reference frame, that would still fit in with your idea of relativism.

Ronnie: I wouldn't even need to mention the second part of my definition—that there exists no absolute standard to adjudicate between reference frames.

Nina: Correct.

Ronnie: In case there were one imperial reference frame of all reference frames, the relativist claim that there is no absolute standard to adjudicate between competing frames would still be true. It would still be true that there are no absolutist standards to adjudicate between reference frames if there were no more than one.

Nina: Correct. To say that there are no absolute frame-independent standards to adjudicate between reference frames would be irrelevant, since there would be no second reference frame to compare with the imperial reference frame.

Ronnie: I agree with that.

A Puzzle of Self-Reference

Adam: You know, Ronnie, there's something contradictory about your view that there is no fact of the matter independent of our reference frame.

Ronnie: What's that?

Adam: It sounds like you're saying that there is a fact of the matter after all. You're saying that the fact of the matter is that no fact of the matter independent of any reference frame exists. Either you're being contradictory or you're making a special exemption of your general claim that there are no facts of the matter.

Ronnie: That's not quite right. My saying that the only facts that there are, are facts constructed within frames, is consistent with my denying that there are frame-independent facts of the matter. My remark that no frame-independent facts exist is, itself, frame-dependent. That's neither contradictory nor does it make an exception of itself.

Adam: OK. But here's maybe a related problem for you, Ronnie. For you even to articulate your relativism, you would have to presume that there is a fact of the matter, independent of any reference frames.

Ronnie: How's that?

Adam: Well, you say that a diversity of reference frames exist, right?

Ronnie: Yes.

Adam: So that's a claim about what exists. It looks like a claim about a frame-independent fact of the matter. The diversity of frames wouldn't show up in the first place unless that diversity itself was frame-independent. In other words, the observation that different reference frames exist at all presupposes that there is a fact of the matter about them, independent of reference frames. In that way, relativism itself presupposes absolutism. You can't even assert your relativism without first transcending it. To affirm that truth is frame-relative, we must rise above frame-relativity altogether.

Ronnie: That argument doesn't work either.

Adam: Why not?

Ronnie: Because you can note that a diversity of frames exists from within a more general reference frame. You don't have to note it from some frame-independent space. You don't have to rise above frame-relativity altogether. "Rising above" doesn't entail frame-independence. You could judge one reference frame to be better than another one for certain purposes and interests without an absolute standard to do so!

Adam: So, with respect to what reference frame would you say your relativism is true?

Ronnie: I would say that it's relative to our context, to our culture, to our time in history.

Adam: I guess that, whether you accept that answer, depends upon whether you find the idea of a reference frame to be coherent. As you know, I continue to have doubts about that.

Barbara: I'm getting a little philosophy-glut. Maybe it's time to turn in. But I am eager to hear whether the three of you might concede that there is room for reconciliation between relativism and absolutism.

Ronnie: That should be interesting. Let's leave that question for tomorrow.

~

Reconciling Relativism and Absolutism

Relative Absolutism or Absolute Relativism

Barbara: I've been thinking about yesterday's discussion and wondering whether relativism and absolutism can somehow be combined. Do they have to oppose each other?

Ronnie: I appreciate your reconciliatory attitude, Barbara, but if there's one thing that Adam and I can agree about, it's that we both can't be right! Don't you agree, Adam?

Adam: I sure do.

Nina: Actually, I think you both could be wrong. If you reject absolutism, that doesn't make you a relativist. Likewise, if you reject relativism, that doesn't make you an absolutist. You could embrace something altogether different in turn, maybe a form of mysticism.

Ronnie: I sure would like to hear about that at some point, Nina. But Barbara thinks we could both be right. Let's hear about that.

Nina: So, Barbara, how can Ronnie and Adam both be right?

Barbara: Well, maybe we could combine some aspects of each of their views. Maybe there's some room for reconciliation. To be sure, both Adam and Ronnie would need to compromise a little to agree on a middle way.

Ronnie: I'm not sure that there's room for reconciliation. Either the truth of a belief, for example, depends upon its place in a reference frame or it doesn't. How can it both depend and not depend upon a reference frame at the same time?

Barbara: Still, maybe we can find a middle way that captures the spirit of each of your views—a way that you both can live with—even uncomfortably.

Ronnie: OK. Let's hear this.

Barbara: As I understand your position, Adam, you believe there are frame-independent facts about the way the world is. You hold that statements are true if they accord with the way the world is, and false if they don't. Their truth or falsity doesn't depend upon anyone's reference frame.

Adam: Yes, that's it.

Barbara: You, Ronnie, believe that all that we know or experience is filtered via some reference frame. We know what we do through some reference frame, and there's no absolutist way to adjudicate between reference frames.

Ronnie: That's right. I don't deny that there's anything there. I couldn't do that. I just say that we have no access to a world of differentiated objects or undifferentiated stuff.

Barbara: OK, then. How about this for reconciliation? How about a *relative absolutism*? Alternatively, how about an *absolute relativism*?

Nina: Those possibilities sound contradictory, but you have me intrigued.

Ronnie: I don't see how my relativism could be absolute.

Adam: Neither can I see how my absolutism could be relative.

Barbara: Well, let's consider relative absolutism first. It's not so very different from Adam's view. Relative absolutists could hold that truth, for example, is absolute. At the same time, they could hold that reference frames limit our access to the way of the world. This combination acknowledges the distinction between ontic and epistemic. It would combine ontic absolutism with epistemic relativism.

Nina: So, what is this distinction between ontic and epistemic?

Barbara: Well, the ontic is the level that concerns what there is, that is, what exists. The epistemic is the level at which we know what there is.

Nina: What you're calling relative absolutism combines relativism at the epistemic level and absolutism at the ontic level, right?

Barbara: Right. Relative absolutism would hold that our knowledge of the world is frame-relative. But there is a fact of the matter about the way the world is. The world is what it is, independent of reference frames. At the same time, reference frames screen our knowledge of it. Our knowledge would be frame-dependent.

Adam: I agree with one part of relative absolutism, but not with another part of it.

Barbara: What part do you agree with?

Adam: I agree that the world is what it is independent of any reference frame. But I don't agree that our knowledge of it has to be screened via some reference frame. I believe that sometimes we do have direct access to it.

Barbara: So you are an ontic absolutist, but you're not an epistemic relativist. You're not what I'm calling a relative absolutist.

Adam: Right.

Barbara: But at least you agree with one part of relative absolutism.

Adam: Yes, only one part.

Nina: But I see that somebody could embrace ontic absolutism and still argue that what we know of the world would be screened via some reference frames. That would be an interesting compromise between absolutism and relativism.

Ronnie: OK, Barbara. What about absolute relativism?

Barbara: Absolute relativism would combine absolutism at the epistemic level and relativism at the ontic level. Absolute relativism would hold that all our knowledge is frame-dependent, but that within that context, it takes some presuppositions as fundamental or most basic, including presuppositions as to what exists. Those presuppositions would be the absolute starting point of an inquiry. They would be absolute within a designated reference frame. They would be like first principles or axioms within a reference frame.

Nina: But Barbara, if those first presuppositions or principles or axioms would be relative to a reference frame, then they wouldn't really be absolute, would they? Maybe they would be absolute in some other sense than frame-independence. Maybe they could be absolute in the sense of being most basic in an inquiry. But that's not the same sense of the term absolute that Adam has been using or the same sense of absolutism in your definition of relative absolutism. It wouldn't signal reference-frame independence.

Barbara: I guess you're right. They would be absolute only in relation to a particular inquiry. That would be another sense of absolute than the one that Adam supports.

Nina: In this context, the word "absolute" would designate a presupposition taken as a given—taken within a frame, like an axiom of a system without assuming that the axiom is true independent of any system.

Barbara: We can fix presuppositions as given, as absolute in regard to an inquiry, say. It would be absolute in this different sense.

Nina: How about an example?

Barbara: OK. Take the geometry case again. There's no fact of the matter whether the shortest distance between two points is a straight line independent of a given geometry. The shortest distance between two points is a straight line in a Euclidean geometry and it isn't in a non-Euclidean geometry, like Riemannian geometry. It depends on what you take as a first principle. There's your absolute relativism.

Ronnie: Nina's right, Barbara. All you're doing in your so-called absolutist relativism is to emphasize that you're taking certain presuppositions as fundamental or basic, except you call it absolute. It's an absolute presupposition within, not independent of a reference frame.

Barbara: True, I realize that when I try to reconcile relativism with absolutism by invoking absolute relativism, I need to change what Adam means by the word "absolute." An absolute relativist is someone who postulates a most fundamental or basic or axiomatic presupposition within a reference frame.

Nina: So, it's more like an "internal absolute" rather than an "external absolute." You mean that the internal absolute view is like saying that one takes particular assumptions as unquestioned or as axiomatic, as a postulation.

Barbara: Yes, you're right. I suppose that does make "absolute relativism" a kind of relativism.

Ronnie: So when you want to reconcile relativism and absolutism you had better be careful not to change meanings of these terms.

Adam: But what kind of reconciliation could it be, if the way you do it is to change the meanings of the terms? I mean, how can relativism and absolutism be reconciled in a so-called absolute relativism when "absolute" doesn't mean the same thing as "absolute" meant before you attempted reconciliation? It's no reconciliation at all, beyond a merely verbal trick. It's just equivocating on the term "absolute." At least relative absolutism—as a form of absolutism—doesn't do that. Relative absolutism says that while our knowledge may be relative to a reference frame, the ontic facts of the matter exist independent of any reference frame. In contrast, absolute relativism is an internal absolutism, which is to say that it's no absolutism at all!

Barbara: Well, if absolute relativism could do any reconciling at all, it would depend upon your agreement to bend the meaning of absolutism. Clearly you're not ready to do that, Adam.

Ontic versus Epistemic

Nina: Adam and Ronnie, you both seem to assume that there are these two levels, namely the ontic—what actually is—and the epistemic—our knowledge of what is. Barbara, your idea of relative absolutism assumes such a distinction.

Adam: Yes, Ronnie and I agree that there is a distinction between what there is and our knowledge about it, don't we?

Ronnie: Yes.

Adam: But we differ about whether sometimes we have access to what there is. Ronnie denies that we have such access.

Ronnie: You understand my position correctly, Adam. I believe that we never have access to the world, because any knowledge we do have is filtered through some reference frame, through some description of what there is. We can know the world only as conceptualized in one way or another. So, when we seek to compare a description of the world with the world itself, we are comparing a description with another description. All we can compare is one description with another description, not a description with the world-as-it-is-in-itself.

Nina: Ronnie, I'm not clear about what you're saying. Are you agreeing with Adam that a frame-independent world exists, but then claiming that human beings have no access to it? Or are you denying the existence of a world altogether?

Ronnie: Again, I'm not sure I need to deny that a frame-independent world exists. Whether one exists doesn't matter. Regardless of whether there is such a world, it can play no functional role in our conduct of inquiry. All we have to work with is what has been processed via a reference frame. All that matters is at the epistemic level. So I can remain agnostic about what you believe we might have access to. We might as well let go of the idea of a frame-independent world. It doesn't matter as regards our conduct of inquiry.

Nina: I still have reservations about the distinction between the ontic and the epistemic. I'm wondering if that distinction is intelligible.

Barbara: How so?

Nina: Well, the idea of the epistemic requires me to contrast it with the ontic. Without the idea of the ontic I couldn't make sense of the idea of the epistemic.

Barbara: And?

Nina: I wonder whether you can even draw the distinction between the world and our knowledge of it. If we do so we have to do it within a reference frame. But it's only within a reference frame that we can make the very idea of what there is intelligible to start with.

Barbara: Say more.

Nina: You can make sense of the distinction between the ontic and the epistemic only within the epistemic. So our conceptualization of the ontic really rests on the epistemic. In that case, though, it seems that the distinction collapses. Yet without the contrast between ontic and epistemic, you couldn't even say, as I just did, that the distinction can operate at the epistemic level only.

Barbara: That's very puzzling.

Nina: I don't think that the distinction between ontic and epistemic is a distinction with a difference. I mean that the distinction makes no functional sense. It doesn't do any work.

Ronnie: I agree. Any knowledge we have about what Adam calls the world is seen via some reference frame. There's no truth except in relation to one or another reference frame.

Adam: But even if you're right, Ronnie, that our knowledge is always interpreted via some reference frame—and I don't believe you're right about that—you also seem to need to mention the idea of the world. I mean, it seems that you already need to have the idea of the world to affirm that our knowledge of the world is gotten via some reference frame. You need to assume the distinction between the ontic and the epistemic.

Ronnie: Well, then maybe I should drop all talk of the world.

Barbara: I can see that even drawing the distinction between ontic and epistemic is controversial. But let's try a different way that we might combine relativism with absolutism. We might do it by values.

Reconciliation by Values

Nina: OK. So how could you combine relativism with absolutism according to different values?

Barbara: Well, take Ronnie's original formulation of relativism. Here it is again. Truth, goodness, or beauty is relative to a reference frame, and no absolute frame-independent ways of adjudicating between reference frames exist. Let's focus on these three values—truth, goodness, and beauty. Now this definition of relativism allows that either some or all of these values could be frame-relative. You could be absolutist as regards truth, for example, but relativist as regards goodness or beauty. You could be absolutist as regards goodness but not as regards truth or beauty. You could be absolutist as regards beauty but not as regards truth or goodness.

Nina: Some of those options would be odd, wouldn't they?

Barbara: Why do you say that? I can imagine someone being an absolutist as regards truth who at the same time holds that goodness is relative to a culture and beauty is relative to a culture. Polygamy, for example, may be judged to be good in one culture and bad in another culture. Along similar lines of reasoning, an artwork or a piece of music might be considered beautiful relative to one's culture and ugly relative to another culture.

Nina: OK. Those combinations don't sound so odd. What about the others?

Barbara: I can imagine someone believing that God mandates what is good, but at the same time believing that truth and beauty are frame-dependent. In turn, I can imagine someone holding that truth and goodness are frame-dependent, but that beauty is not frame-dependent, accessible perhaps only to special people who have a highly developed aesthetic sensibility. They just see beauty wherever it is.

Nina: I guess I see—at least in formal terms—how you might be piece-meal in applying relativism and absolutism to those values. But you'd have to say a lot more about making those positions plausible, especially those positions which make goodness and beauty frame-independent. It's one thing to imagine someone holding those different positions. It's something else to say that they really are plausible.

Barbara: I don't know about their plausibility. It just seems that there are those formal possibilities in regard to the values mentioned in Ronnie's original definition of relativism.

Adam: Right. I just don't see how anybody could plausibly be relativist as regards truth, for example, and be absolutist as regards goodness or beauty. I mean, even to say that a given act is good presupposes it's true that it is good. Even to say that a given artwork or a piece of music is beautiful presupposes that it's true that it's beautiful.

Ronnie: So, Adam, you think that if you're relativist as regards truth you can't be absolutist about goodness or beauty. And if you're absolutist as regards truth, you can't be relativist about goodness or beauty. Whatever your view of truth is, it's got to carry over to your view of goodness or beauty.

Adam: Yes.

Barbara: But maybe all we mean by good acts or beautiful things is that they make us feel good. Maybe our view of truth doesn't have to carry over to goodness or beauty. Anyhow, I can see that a lot more would need to be said to make the piecemeal approach to truth, goodness, and beauty plausible. In any case, it's interesting to note that those values of truth, goodness, and beauty look like they are bivalent.

Bivalence

Nina: What do you mean by that, Barbara?

Barbara: We typically assume that truth opposes falsity. It's the same thing with goodness and beauty. We typically mean to contrast good with bad, or beautiful with ugly. They appear to exclude one another.

Nina: What are you getting at, Barbara?

Barbara: Here's the thing. The negation of each amounts to the affirmation of the other. When you negate true, you get false. When you negate good, you get bad. When you negate beautiful, you get ugly. They are like a standard on-off light switch.

Nina: So?

Barbara: Well, a lot of the time we don't actually talk about things that way. Sometimes we say that a belief is reasonable or unreasonable instead of true or false. Or, an action might be appropriate or inappropriate. Or, a work of art could be inspiring or uninspiring.

Nina: And?

Barbara: Being reasonable isn't bivalent. When we say that it's reasonable to believe that the earth rotates around the sun, that doesn't disallow saying that it's reasonable to say that the sun rotates around the earth. Both claims could be reasonable. Reasonableness works differently from bivalent truth or falsity. While a belief may be reasonable, its opposite can also be considered reasonable.

Reasonable persons can disagree. Sometimes we talk in bivalent terms. Other times we talk in multivalent terms.

Nina: This is interesting. Say more.

Barbara: Well, two opposed judgments may be reasonable. So a hypothesis may be true and reasonable, true and unreasonable, false and reasonable, and false and unreasonable. Appropriateness and inappropriateness may apply to a given action. There are other multivalent values that work that way too—for example, praise-worthiness and unpraiseworthiness, or fairness and unfairness, or an artwork's or an action's capacity to inspire.

Adam: I don't get any of that. Reasonableness is also bivalent—as is appropriateness, praiseworthiness, fairness, or the capability to inspire. If someone says that a hypothesis is reasonable and the next person says that it's unreasonable, that means either that one of them is wrong, or that each is referring to different aspects of the hypothesis. You can't have it both ways. The same applies for the other cases.

Barbara: Adam, wait. Sure, truth is bivalent. Its negation is falsity, and vice versa. But not all values are like truth in that way. Upon meeting a friend, shaking hands is appropriate. But that doesn't mean that not doing so is inappropriate. Volunteering for a just military or political campaign may be praiseworthy or inspiring. But not doing so need not be unpraiseworthy or uninspiring. If raising taxes—say, to educate young people—is fair, that doesn't mean that not raising taxes for that purpose is unfair.

Ronnie: I agree with you, Barbara.

Reconciliation by Domains

Nina: So, Barbara, can you suggest any other ways to reconcile Adam's absolutism and Ronnie's relativism?

Barbara: Try this. You could parse domains. I mean you could apply relativism in one domain and absolutism in another domain. I can imagine someone holding to absolutism in the cognitive domain, but relativism in the moral and aesthetic domains. Or one could be absolutist in the moral domain, but relativist in the cognitive and aesthetic domains. Or one could be absolutist in the aesthetic domain but relativist in the cognitive and moral domains—all rather parallel to the combinations in regard to the values of truth, goodness, and beauty that we already mentioned.

Nina: I see why this reconciliation by domains differs from reconciliation by values. Those values might not uniquely apply to some of those domains that you might at first expect them to.

Barbara: What do you mean?

Nina: Well, I can imagine that in the aesthetic domains—where we are concerned with works of art, music, or literature—we might want to make claims of truth. In the scientific domain—where we are concerned with empirical theories and tests—we might want to make claims of beauty. Maybe we observe that a theory is beautiful or that we prefer one or another hypothesis because one is simpler than another. That's also true in the moral domain where we are concerned with relations between persons. We might want to make claims of beauty there too.

Barbara: OK. Then let's say that the values of truth, goodness, and beauty can apply in a piecemeal way to different domains, without assuming that those values uniquely range over those domains. You could parse relativism or absolutism over different domains. If each of those domains were distinct, that might be a way to combine relativism and absolutism.

Nina: That's interesting. But I wonder if it could work.

Barbara: Why shouldn't it?

Nina: Well, I'm wondering about that qualification you mentioned.

Barbara: What qualification?

Nina: You suggested that we might be absolutist in one domain and relativist in another—if, that is, they are distinct. What if they're not distinct? What if your views in one domain carry over to other domains? Ronnie talks about reference frames in terms of which we see the world. That sounds like they are like lenses for anything we experience.

Barbara: What do you mean?

Nina: Well when I wear my glasses, for example, they're still on my nose when I look at you, when I look at this teacup, when I look at the Ganges, or whatever.

Barbara: What's your point, Nina?

Nina: Well, if our understanding is always filtered somehow, it seems that it's filtered regardless of what we look at. That suggests that if we're relativists, we have to be relativists across the board. Otherwise, we'd have to take off our glasses when we're looking at certain things and put them on when we're looking at other things. That would be strange.

Barbara: But I'm not so sure about that, Nina. Some people have different glasses, depending on what they're looking at. Some people put on glasses for some things, and don't use glasses at all for other sorts of things. Why does it have to be an all-or-nothing thing?

Nina: But nobody has different glasses for every particular thing they see! Nobody has special glasses to look at particular teacups and other special glasses to look at particular rivers, or special glasses to look at particular boats, for example.

Ronnie: But you know what? We all wear glasses all the time. We all have lenses in our eyes. In addition to that, the brain interprets what it receives from our optical nerves. We never can just see what is before us to start with.

Nina: What's interesting about Adam's absolutism is that things are what they are without glasses, and according to him, sometimes we can see them for what they are without glasses. On the other hand, Ronnie's relativism asserts that we never can see without glasses. We need glasses all the time. But the piecemeal approach won't work if conclusions we draw about one domain carry over to other domains—if, that is, the arguments for reference frame-dependence we apply in one domain apply to all domains.

Adam: That's a big if. Let's look at that. I'm an absolutist about truth. That's what we're calling a cognitive absolutist, right?

Nina: Yes.

Adam: So Barbara's idea is that I could be a cognitive absolutist and a moral relativist, for example.

Barbara: Yes, that's right.

Adam: When I say that truth is absolute, and I say it's true that one should not steal, for example, I'm being a cognitivist with respect to a moral judgment. Or, if I say it's true that the Taj Mahal is beautiful, then I'm a cognitivist with regard to an aesthetic judgment. I'm saying that it's true. So, if I'm a cognitive absolutist, that position would dispose me toward being an absolutist across the board.

Nina: That's an interesting argument for being global about your absolutism. But I'm wondering about your assumption that we need to be cognitivists across the board.

Barbara: What do you have in mind, Nina?

Nina: Maybe sometimes, when we say things such as, you should not steal, that really amounts to saying, "Don't do that!" It's a directive, an injunction. Or when we say that that painting is beautiful, maybe all we mean is "Wow!" or "Cool!" or "Awesome!" Maybe those remarks aren't cognitive. Maybe they don't really involve truth at all.

Adam: So you mean that my temptation to include all domains under the cognitive banner might not work?

Nina: I mean that sometimes, when we are concerned with morality or aesthetics, for example, what looks like a cognitive claim—a claim of truth—might not really be a cognitive claim. It may just be an expression of approval or disapproval. That's all.

Domains and Their Kinds

Nina: I'm wondering whether there is a fact of the matter about what distinguishes one domain from another.

Adam: Barbara's been talking about domains—cognitive, moral, and aesthetic. It seems that for her to do so, she needs to assume that those domains exist, and that a natural cut between them exists.

Nina: That's an interesting point.

Adam: She would have to be an absolutist at that deeper level. She would have to hold that cognitive, moral, aesthetic, and perhaps other domains exist irrespective of reference frames.

Ronnie: But she could say that those domains, rather than being independent of reference frames, are dependent upon them. She could say that those domains are made, not found—not given, but taken. She could say that the distinctions between them are human achievements.

Nina: Adam, you seem to believe that designated domains reflect distinct joints inherent in the world, as if distinct differences between domains exist quite apart from how humans categorize things.

Ronnie: But it's by way of convention that we slice up the domains. The difference between the domains is conventional.

Nina: So, Ronnie, you don't believe any inherent difference in kind exists, say, between science, morality, and art? There's no inherent difference between those and religion, history, and, say, philosophy? Are those differences merely a matter of our purposes and interests, a matter of convention?

Ronnie: Sure, there are obvious differences between religion and science, for example. But I don't see why those differences can't be accommodated within the terms of reference frames. We don't need to go so far as to say that natural kinds exist absolutely to allow that different kinds exist within reference frames.

Barbara: So, Ronnie, how would your global relativism apply to different domains such as history or religion?

Nina: Yes. What about history?

Ronnie: There is no fact of the matter independent of all reference frames. Even if there were, it wouldn't make any difference. We couldn't have access to them. Everything we know is frame-relative. That applies to history too.

Adam: What do you mean? Take the fact that India became an independent nation in 1947.

Ronnie: I don't dispute that it took place then.

Adam: Well, at least we agree about that.

Ronnie: But I'm not sure our understanding of our agreement is the same.

Adam: What do you mean?

Ronnie: Well, that claim is an interpreted claim. It's a matter of interpretation what India is. It's a matter of interpretation what an independent nation is. It's a matter of interpretation what 1947 is.

Adam: What? I can't believe what you're saying. Are you saying that you don't believe that Independence took place then?

Ronnie: Don't get me wrong! I acknowledge that there was a day of independence in 1947. All I'm saying is that that truth is a matter of interpretation.

Adam: I don't understand how you can say that truth is a matter of interpretation.

Ronnie: Well, if you don't allow that interpreted claims can be true, then nothing that we believe can be true, because all that we believe is interpreted. After the event, after the fact, historians assign significance to an event by virtue of what they deem to be significant in a present narrative. That's what written history is about. We decide that certain events were significant because they gave rise to significant consequences in the present.

Adam: But you're also saying that what—at the time—actually happened is frame-relative. That sounds strange to me. I believe that a fact of the matter about what happened exists. Assigning significance to a fact of the matter requires a fact of the matter to start with. You can have interpretation. But you need description of the fact of the matter to start with.

Ronnie: Think about it. You say that you were born on September 13, 1980, say, at 1:07 p.m. You may even think you know the second, say at 1:07 p.m. and 18 seconds. You know that's true. But it's not frame-independent. You have indirect evidence that you were born then. A birth certificate may be evidence that that is when you were born. But you have no access to a frame-independent fact of the matter, do you?

Adam: What do you mean?

Ronnie: What calendar are you assuming—the Gregorian calendar in contrast to maybe the Hebrew or Hindu, or Chinese or Egyptian or Roman calendars? For that matter, 1:07 p.m. in what time zone?

Adam: I'm using the Gregorian calendar. I was born in California, that's in the Pacific Time zone.

Ronnie: That's a reference frame.

Adam: It's one thing to say that what a historian writes about involves selection and judgments of significance. It's another thing to say that what actually happened depends upon what a historian believes is important.

Ronnie: I don't believe that facts are given. What you call facts are taken, and they are taken in light of reference frames. Your so-called facts are always already interpreted via some interpretive reference frame. That's especially true in the case of history.

Barbara: Ronnie, I see that you're being consistent about your global relativism. You believe that it holds across the board, that it applies to all domains—that it applies to what there is as well as to our knowledge of what there is.

Ronnie: Yes. My relativism is global. The reasons for its applying in one domain also apply to all domains.

Barbara: That's because all our knowledge is, in your view, interpreted knowledge via some reference frame. Moreover, if I understand your position correctly, even if there were facts of the matter—if that makes any sense at all according to you—we could have no access to them.

Ronnie: That's pretty much it.

Morality and Human Life

Nina: Ronnie, I see that you mean for your relativism to apply across the board—for all domains. So, how does it apply to moral cases?

Ronnie: OK. Take the now-outlawed Indian practice of sati—where a grieving widow would throw herself into the funeral pyre in which her husband was being cremated. She would do that to assure her continued union with her deceased husband in the next life. My global relativism applies to those sorts of cases too.

Barbara: That's a terrible practice!

Nina: Yes, we might agree that it's terrible. But it was a fairly common practice—especially in rural areas—until the Indian government made it illegal in 1987. But, you know, it's still practiced in some remote areas.

Adam: So, Ronnie, what do you say about that? Would you say that, in accord with your global relativism, that it's all right for some communities to pursue that practice? Would you say that sati is morally right for them and morally wrong for us?

Ronnie: I think that practice *is* awful.

Adam: But you can't go so far as to say that sati is *morally wrong* as such, can you?

Ronnie: No, I can't. But I can be as firm as anyone else about rejecting it and criticizing the practice. At the same time, my criticism will inevitably be cast within the terms of my reference frame. For me to find it repugnant does not require your absolutist assumption that there is a moral fact of the matter, independent of all reference frames. All I know, including moral knowledge, is frame-dependent.

Nina: So I guess you'd have to go still further and to say that the value of human life itself is frame-dependent.

Ronnie: Yes. It goes back to the idea that, what it is to be human is, itself, frame–dependent, relative to a particular level of description. Since there's no fact of the matter as to what it is to be human, there's no fact of the matter as to what a human life is, and there's no fact of the matter as to the quality of human life.

Adam: What?

Ronnie: Don't get me wrong. I'm not saying those things don't exist. Rather, I'm saying that they do exist within a reference frame. For something to exist, it need not exist independent of any frame. Remember that being human—in contrast to being a bundle of electrons in space—is frame-relative. So is the value of human life. We assign, rather than discover, an extremely high value to human life. That's why I abhor the practice of sati. Yet it's on account of our affirmation that it is basic to us—to us as humans, within the reference frame of the human—that human life has that high value.

Adam: So, Ronnie, you believe that the value of human life derives from taking it as such, rather than from its being given as such. It's like what Barbara called absolute relativism. You believe that we take human life as most basic. You postulate it as axiomatic. But still, it's no fact of the matter independent of frames.

Ronnie: Yes, that's my view.

Intervention

Nina: So, Ronnie, do you believe we should ever intervene in another's culture? Should we ever impose our values on people of another culture? If there are no absolute standards that cross cultures, maybe we shouldn't intervene.

Ronnie: Some people might believe that, because our knowledge is frame-dependent, we shouldn't criticize or intervene in other cultures. I don't see it that way. Criticism and intervention can be important—critically important. Just because our knowledge is frame-dependent shouldn't silence us or keep us from intervening if necessary.

Barbara: Of course, the Indian government has intervened and has made sati illegal. Do you believe that it was right for it to do so, Ronnie?

Ronnie: Yes, they were right, from their reference frame, as articulated, say, by the United Nations' Universal Declaration of Human Rights. They're not coming from a frame-independent place.

Adam: But Ronnie, when you say that it was right for the Indian government to do so, aren't you saying it was inherently right? Doesn't the United Nations' Universal Declaration of Human Rights present itself as an absolutist statement? Doesn't it mean to assert the inherent existence of human rights independently of reference frames?

Ronnie: Actually, if you read the U.N. Declaration carefully, it's not so clear that it does present itself as an absolutist document. It speaks of itself as a covenant, as an *agreement* to be accepted universally. The U.N.'s Declaration is just that. It declares what it takes to be human rights. Those rights need not be thought to be givens, but takens. By declaring, they were installing the rights. So, I'm saying that it was right for the Indian government to intervene according to its reference frame.

Adam: But what if the criticisms against sati, for example, were not heeded?

Ronnie: I see no reason why the Indian government shouldn't have intervened. They imposed their views on the people who practiced sati. Sometimes they still practice sati even though it's illegal.

Nina: So you think that your relativism doesn't rule out criticism or even intervention.

Ronnie: That's right.

Adam: Well, I'm relieved to hear that your relativism doesn't rule those out. But I'd be happier if criticism or intervention were based upon our knowledge of moral facts of the matter, and not filtered through some reference frame. So, Ronnie, I'm still troubled by your moral relativism. Take the case of al-Qaeda. They believe that it's morally acceptable to engage in suicide bombing. According to our morality, it's morally unacceptable to do so. But we can't just leave it at that. There's got to be a moral fact of the matter beyond our reference frames that can adjudicate between our views.

Ronnie: I'm as outraged as you are about such practices. But our question is, "What conceptual resources do we have to justify our outrage?"

Adam: I say that suicide bombing is inherently immoral, period. You say it's immoral relative to some reference frame.

Ronnie: Correct. It's immoral given that we have taken the preservation of innocent lives as axiomatic.

Adam: But that's impossibly permissive.

Ronnie: Wait a minute. It's not permissive. It's right for the Allied Forces to rout out al-Qaeda and other terrorists.

Adam: But your sense of right is too weak, isn't it?

Ronnie: Why?

Adam: You would have to say that Allied interventions are right for us.

Ronnie: Yes.

Adam: But turn the situation around. What if al-Qaeda's people were to say that it's right for them to engage in suicide bombings and to kill innocent civilians? That's what they take as axiomatic. There has to be a stronger basis to assert the moral wrongness of these sorts of acts. It can't just be a matter of reference frame-dependence.

Ronnie: To say that no absolutes exist, doesn't entail that there are no good reasons for embracing one morality over another. My ability to have good reasons to intervene doesn't require that those reasons must be frame-independent. That's my point! It's in our best interests to intervene.

Adam: But for you to have good reasons for favoring one morality over another requires some frame-independent moral principles. Otherwise, your whole moral structure has no force.

Ronnie: It has limited force, limited to one's reference frame. Sometimes it's enough. Other times, it's not.

Barbara: Even if our own reference frame limits us, we can have meaningful conversations with others of different reference frames. I mean intervention doesn't have to involve an assertion of power.

Ronnie: What do you have in mind, Barbara?

Barbara: Take the case of al-Qaeda again. I think we could have a meaningful conversation with some of their people.

Ronnie: What would that look like?

Barbara: Well, we might ask if they believe that their strategies are counter-productive to their own ends. We might ask an al-Qaeda leader, for example, if, in the end, he hopes for a peaceful resolution. We might ask whether he believes that, if India were to attack Pakistan, his threat to send suicide bombers to India is in his best interest. How sure is he that Pakistan is his ally? Does he realize that such a threat might fuel a never-ending cycle of violence? We might ask if such a threat fosters his ultimate aim for peace—if that is his aim to start with. In other words, we can have conversation and negotiation between parties, even if they are constrained by reference fames.

Adam: That's all very wishful thinking, Barbara. It assumes that peoples of different reference frames, in the end, share overlapping purposes and interests. If they don't, there's not much hope for progress in such conversations, is there?

Barbara: I'm not saying they will always succeed. But it's definitely worth a try. It's worth prodding one another to see if they—and we—really do wish for our peoples to live happy productive lives.

An Aesthetic Example

Nina: Let's take a step back. We've been talking about possible ways to reconcile relativism and absolutism, maybe by parsing different domains. According to that strategy, somebody might hold to absolutism in the cognitive domain, but relativism in the moral and aesthetic domains, for example.

Barbara: Right. What about the aesthetic domain? How does your global relativism apply there, Ronnie?

Ronnie: I'd say pretty much the same thing there as I have said for the moral domain.

Barbara: Can you give us an example?

Ronnie: Sure. Some people say that the proportions exhibited in the cross section of the chambered nautilus shell, for example, exemplify aesthetically perfect proportions. They believe that they reflect something independent of reference frames.

Barbara: What are those proportions?

Ronnie: Well according to the Fibonacci number series, aesthetically perfect proportions can be formalized into particular numerical ratios. Take this series—0, 1, 1, 2, 3, 5, 8, 13, 21, and so on.

Barbara: What's special about this series?

Ronnie: The first two numbers are 0 and 1. After that, any number is the sum of the previous two numbers. The idea is that the rib of the shell expands exactly according to the Fibonacci series. The amazing thing is that it has been observed to apply not just to the chambered nautilus, but also to all kinds of other beautiful things such as snowflakes and the spiral florets at the center of the sunflower.

Barbara: I'd imagine that an absolutist concerned with the aesthetic domain would be happy with those examples. It could be taken to show that beauty is frame-independent, that beauty is a fact of the matter, a given and not something imposed onto it.

Adam: Yes, I was about to say the same thing, Barbara.

Ronnie: But, however beautiful the nautilus series or snowflakes or sunflowers are, it doesn't show that their proportions reflect an aesthetic fact of the matter independent of all frames. It's one thing to say that those things exhibit the Fibonacci proportions. It's another thing to say that it captures what beauty inherently is. The series does not establish that there is anything about those proportions that captures an aesthetic frame-independent fact of the matter.

Absolutism and Relativism in the Religious Domain

Nina: I can see how Barbara's idea of parsing relativism and absolutism according to domains might be thought to apply. Let's move on to the religious domain. I'm particularly interested in that. I can imagine someone urging that, at least in the case of religion, some people have direct experience of an absolute divinity. The divine is revealed to them.

Ronnie: I can imagine someone making such a claim. But to be convincing, they'd have to provide the basis on which it can be defended. I mean, they'd have to show how they would have such access. In contrast, a religious relativist could hold that a person or text is holy or unholy, righteous or unrighteous, relative to a reference frame.

Nina: I don't think you can be relativist about religion. If we consider the Abrahamic traditions—Judaism, Christianity, and Islam—they all believe that there is an omniscient creator God. They hold that their belief is absolutely true. They don't believe that their belief is only relatively true for them. Regarding knowledge of that fact, they believe that prophets and other religious persons have direct access to that fact as such. They believe that they do so through revelation—quite independent of any reference frames at all. So they would be absolutist at the ontological level and absolutist at the epistemic level.

Ronnie: I'm more sympathetic than you might think. I don't doubt that some religious Jews, Christians, and Muslims believe what you say they believe. But whatever they believe must be frame-relative, and how they know what they know must be frame-relative as well. Yet, I don't believe that such notions as the holy or the divine are empty of content. I think that such notions might be made intelligible within reference frames. Holiness and divinity don't need to be understood in absolutist terms. So, if holiness and divinity is the core of what religious people wish to preserve, then there is room for them in my relativist view. I know that's not the usual Abrahamic view, but it's not inconsistent with relativism.

Adam: But such a relativist construction would misrepresent the views of a lot of religious Jews, Christians, and Muslims. They believe that their claim of an omniscient creator God is absolutely true. As an absolutist, I believe that their claim is absolutely true, or absolutely false. For myself, I don't know which it is. I'm still an agnostic on that point. But either it's true or false in an absolute sense.

Nina: We've been talking about Abrahamic religions. But if we consider Hinduism and Buddhism, for example, we get a different picture. In Hinduism and Buddhism alike, the idea of a creator God doesn't appear.

Adam: My absolutism, as it applies to the religious domain, would have to hold there too. On the one hand, religious Jews, Christians, and Muslims are absolutely right or absolutely wrong to believe that a creator God exists. On the other hand, Hindus and Buddhists are absolutely right or absolutely wrong to believe that a creator God doesn't exist. Whichever it is—and, as I say, I don't know which it is—it's got to be an absolute fact of the matter.

Nina: But can you know which it is? Can anyone know which it is?

Barbara: I suppose that depends upon your view of revelation or something of that sort.

Nina: Someone might insist that Hinduism or Buddhism is absolutely right or wrong in a frame-independent sense. Yet Hinduism and Buddhism sometimes use the words—absolute and relative—in a somewhat different sense. Sometimes by absolute they mean something that is beyond either frame-dependent or frame-independent.

Barbara: What would that be?

Nina: The fundamental or basic assumption of Hinduism is the inherent existence of Atman—or Oneness. It's inherent because all that exists is reducible to it, and it is not itself further reducible. It's the Ultimate Reality.

Barbara: What about Buddhism?

Nina: Yes. The Tibetan Buddhist, for example, claims that ultimately nothing exists inherently—or that nothing is inherently understood. They hold that there can be no inherent Atma. That means that all that exists or is understandable is relative to some conventional reference frame.

Barbara: Is there any way to reconcile the Hindu and the Buddhist views?

Nina: That might be possible in a limited way. I mean, both the Hindu and the Buddhist agree that the conventional or the relative level doesn't capture the ultimate nature of things. They differ, of course, in that the Hindu asserts that ultimately—beyond the relative level—there is the inherent Oneness: Atman. For their part, Buddhists hold that there's no inherent anything. But at least both agree that at the relative level—all is conventional and therefore not inherent. For the Hindu, there's an ultimate inherent Atman. For the Buddhist, there is no ultimate inherent anything.

Ronnie: Before we get too involved with the Hindu and Buddhist cases, maybe it's a good idea to recall why Barbara wanted us to consider all these different general domains—the cognitive, moral, aesthetic, and other domains.

Barbara: OK. Ronnie. As you know, I'm looking for a way to reconcile Adam's kind of absolutism with Ronnie's kind of relativism. I've suggested that maybe we could just parse absolutism and relativism over different domains.

Adam: I'm sympathetic with your reconciliatory attitude, Barbara. But you know, I still think there's an underlying barrier to your doing it—at least according to parsing over domains.

Barbara: Again, why is that?

Adam: Because the very idea of a domain is problematic. Beside the question of what you would count as inside or outside a given domain, there's the question of how you would construe the very idea of a domain itself.

Barbara: What do you have in mind, Adam?

Adam: Well, it seems to me that the idea of a domain is controversial. According to my absolutism, I'd have to say that a domain is there. It exists independent of reference frames. Domains are there, to be discovered and not made. On the other hand, if I understand

Ronnie's relativism rightly, he thinks those domains are frame-dependent, constituted according to certain human purposes and interests. Given that disagreement between us about the idea of domains, I don't see how we could reconcile our views by saying that some domains might answer to my absolutism and other domains would answer to Ronnie's relativism. The idea of domains seems to underlie Barbara's attempt at reconciliation, but we don't seem to agree about how to understand domains to start with. Don't you agree, Ronnie?

Ronnie: Yes. I agree, Adam. Barbara's attempt to reconcile our positions—at least according to parsing by domains—seems thwarted because of the very idea of domains.

Barbara: OK. I tried. But you know what? I'm beginning to think that maybe it's time for us to reconsider the whole question of what we mean by relativism and absolutism.

Nina: I think that's an excellent idea. Let's revisit that question tomorrow.

Ronnie: Great. Till tomorrow then!

~

Strands of Absolutism and Relativism

Self-Refutation of Relativism and the Refinement of Definitions

Nina: I really appreciate your effort to somehow reconcile relativism and absolutism, Barbara. But you know, I don't think we're all that clear about what absolutism is. Until we're clear about that, we won't be clear about what relativism is.

Adam: Nina, I agree with you about that.

Ronnie: Who knows? Maybe if we get still clearer about the meaning of absolutism and relativism, relativists won't be stymied by the old argument against relativism that says it's self-refuting.

Barbara: Remind us of that old argument, Ronnie, would you? Maybe you can refresh our memories from our Canaday College days.

Ronnie: Sure. It goes something like this. Suppose that I say that relativism is true. Then you ask, well, if it's true, in what sense are you saying it's true? Is relativism true in an absolute sense or is it true in a relative sense? Clearly, if I say it's absolutely true, then I'd be contradicting myself. That's the first part of the argument. On the other hand, to avoid the contradiction, I might say that relativism is relatively true. Then you'd ask, relative to what? Then I'd say, relative to a reference frame. Then you'd say, well then your relativism wouldn't be very convincing to anyone who doesn't share your reference frame, would it? That's the second part of the argument. Right now, I'm mostly concerned with the first part of the argument.

Barbara: So, besides getting clearer about the meanings of absolutism and relativism for their own sake, why do you think that we need to get clearer about their meanings just now?

Ronnie: Because if we get more precise about their meanings, the first part of the self-refuting argument might fall away.

Nina: Let's see then. We've been thinking about relativism as a negation of absolutism, and absolutism as a negation of relativism, right?

Barbara: Yes, we have.

Nina: But it now seems to me that absolutism has several strands that are often woven together. They are often conflated.

Barbara: What are you getting at, Nina?

Nina: Well, if we pull apart the strands of absolutism, and since we define relativism in terms of the negation of absolutism, I think we'll find that relativism also has several strands. It might also turn out that some of the strands associated with relativism and some of the strands associated with absolutism might even be compatible, while others are not.

Barbara: So, Nina, you think that we might, after all, combine some strands of relativism and some strands of absolutism?

Nina: Yes.

Barbara: So we had better pull apart the strands to see how they relate.

Nina: Yes. Actually, I think there are three strands of absolutism. And you know what? If a relativist were to negate any one or all of them, the relativist wouldn't be committing a logical contradiction.

Ronnie: Boy, I hope you're right, Nina.

Barbara: OK then. Let's hear how you'd separate the strands of absolutism and the strands of relativism. What are those strands?

Realism, Universalism, and Foundationalism

Nina: Different people emphasize different things when they speak of absolutism. Some emphasize realism, others emphasize universalism, and some emphasize foundationalism. We've actually already been talking about these three things, without explicitly giving them those labels.

Barbara: What's realism?

Nina: Adam has been talking mostly about realism. It's the view that there are facts of the matter independent of reference frames and they are knowable.

Barbara: OK. That's one strand.

Nina: In addition to realism, there's universalism. Universalism holds that all peoples share some important common traits. That's the second strand. For example, Adam has talked as if facts of the matter exist for everyone, and that all persons can have access to them. That's an example of universalism. At the ontic level, universalists hold that what exists does so for all peoples. Moreover, at the epistemic level, universalists hold that all peoples can know what exists. Universalism can be exemplified at both or either of the ontic and the epistemic levels.

Barbara: OK. So what's foundationalism?

Nina: Well, again, Adam has been talking about facts of the matter as if they are inherent or intrinsic. That's foundationalism. At the

ontic level, foundationalism holds that there is a most fundamental inherent constituent of reality. It claims that there must be an
ultimate constituent of what there is, to which everything else is
reducible. It goes beyond the idea that there just is a fact of the
matter beyond reference frames. It says that facts of the matter are
there—inherently, irreducibly, intrinsically. They are not further
analyzable or reducible.

Barbara: Go on.

Nina: At the epistemic level, foundationalism asserts that our knowledge is grounded in first principles that are incapable of further
analysis. It supposes that there must be some most basic, rock
bottom, unanalyzable starting point. There must be an end to
any justification without which you would go on forever. It posits
a self-evident, bedrock condition of self-justification. First principles are self-evident and self-justifying.

Barbara: So what would that look like?

Nina: Take the laws of logic, such as the law of non-contradiction. P or
not-P, but not both P and not-P. A thing can't be itself and not
itself at the same time in the same respect. If you don't embrace
such laws as self-evident, inherent building blocks of thought,
then you can't think or you can't think rationally. Someone who
embraces that idea is a foundationalist at the epistemic level.

Barbara: Can you give some other examples of foundationalism and how
they relate to realism and universalism?

Nina: Sure. I can think of different kinds of cases. We already considered
the idea that what there is, physically, cannot be further reduced
beyond a certain point. This table may be thought to be reducible,
say, to atoms or to subatomic particles. But if someone identifies
particular tiny bits as inherent or intrinsic and not further reducible, that would be foundational. If someone says that there are
moral principles that are inherent or intrinsic and not further reducible, that would be foundationalist. If someone says that there
are inherent properties for beauty, that would be foundational.
Those examples would be relevant at the ontic level. Now at the

epistemic level, if someone says that there are first principles that are inherent for our understanding of anything at all or are inherent to rationality itself, that would be foundational.

Barbara: What about sticks and stones?

Nina: OK. A realist could say that sticks and stones are frame-independent. But he could add that sticks and stones are the sorts of objects that ultimately constitute the world. These are middle-sized objects and they are irreducible. That would make him a foundationalist as well as a realist.

Barbara: But that would be silly. Sticks and stones are composed of other constituents.

Nina: OK, then, if it's not sticks and stones—that is, middle-sized objects—that are irreducible, he might say that other things are, ultimately and inherently, what there is. Foundationalism is the claim that there is some ultimate constituent of what the world is made of. That's foundationalism at the ontic level.

Barbara: But you could deny that there's an ultimate constituent out of which everything else is made. You could keep unpacking constituents of constituents indefinitely. You could ask, "What are electrons made of?" "What are photons made of?" and on and on. The question is always there, regardless whether you've really gotten down to the ultimate constituent.

Nina: Yes. The foundationalist says that there is an ultimate constituent. The non-foundationalist says that there is no such thing as an ultimate constituent.

Ronnie: So, if you say that sticks and stones exist, you assume that they do so as middle-sized objects. If you say, for example, that carbon is a constituent of sticks, for example, you're saying they exist as molecules. If you say that the molecules are composed of electrons, you're saying that electrons exist as subatomic particles, and so on. When you do this, you designate a reference frame in which what you say exists, does so. By doing that, you see that even to say that anything exists at all is frame-dependent.

Barbara: I agree.

Ronnie: So, any description we give of anything presupposes some reference frame. That includes this table, its molecules, its atoms, its electrons, its quarks, and so on. We can't come to an ultimate inherent level.

Nina: Yes. That's non-foundationalism.

Barbara: Can you give another sort of example of the difference between foundationalism and non-foundationalism?

Nina: OK. Consider this. All persons have birth mothers. I expect everyone would agree with that. But a non-foundationalist could say that a person doesn't have to have a birth mother. In that case, having a birth mother wouldn't be an inherent feature of being a person. A human person might be artificially produced without having had a mother who gave birth to it.

Barbara: Wow, what a thought.

Nina: It's not that farfetched given all of the reproductive technology that's going on these days.

Barbara: So what are you driving at?

Nina: Well, if you can imagine persons without birth mothers, then having a birth mother would not be inherent or intrinsic to being a person. If you can imagine that, then—even though all persons have birth mothers now—it wouldn't be intrinsic or inherent that all persons have birth mothers.

Barbara: Oh, I see. So not all universals would have to be inherent.

Nina: That's it. Not all universals need to be foundational.

Barbara: So, more generally, a non-foundationalist would say that, what we call a person resists any inherent properties to be a person. On the other hand, if you're a foundationalist, you'd think that, to be a person, you'd have to embody some inherent properties.

Nina: Right.

Adam: These examples of foundationalism and universalism are interesting. But where is all this going? Again, why is it that we're running through all these examples of realism, universalism, and foundationalism? What's the over-all point you mean to make by mentioning these examples?

Nina: Right. These examples are intriguing in their own right. But the point I'm making concerns the strands or meanings of absolutism. If, by absolutism, you mean any one or a combination of these, and then you negate one or a number of them, it turns out that the negations of realism, universalism, or foundationalism are not self-contradictory. Non-realism is not self-contradictory. Non-universalism is not self-contradictory. Non-foundationalism is not self-contradictory. Whatever else they are, they are not self-contradictory. Remember, the traditional argument against relativism is that it's self-contradictory. But if you disambiguate the idea of absolutism and look at each one of these possible strands or meanings of absolutism, a relativist might negate one or all of them. Yet his doing so wouldn't result in self-contradiction. That's the overriding point.

Adam: OK. I see that. It's worth hearing still more cases how a realist, universalist, or foundationalist construal might apply. Let's hear more.

Ronnie: I have another example. Take the claim that all cultures have and appreciate music of some sort. This example would amount to a foundational universalism if it were tied to the claim that having and appreciating music is an inherent or intrinsic or ultimate feature of being a culture.

Barbara: Yes. But depending upon circumstances, it could be otherwise.

Nina: If you say that, then you'd be non-foundational about that trait.

Barbara: So universalism alone does not necessitate foundational universalism.

Nina: That's what I mean. Peoples of all cultures may appreciate music of one kind or another, but that may not be inherent. So, not all universal characteristics are necessarily foundational. Universalism might be foundational or non-foundational. Foundational universalism holds that all cultures share some common characteristics by virtue of what—irreducibly and ultimately—it is to be a culture. Non-foundational universalism holds that all cultures share common characteristics without presuming that they do so by virtue of what—irreducibly and ultimately—it is to be a culture. Foundational universalism is a claim of necessity while non-foundational universalism is a claim of contingency. Universalism need not be foundational.

Moral Cases

Ronnie: OK, Nina. So, what about moral cases? How do the realist, universalist, and foundationalist strands of absolutism apply there? Take the case of human rights again.

Nina: Realists, in regard to human rights, would say that such rights are given. They exist independent of reference frames. Non-realists would say that they are takens. They exist by virtue of reference frames. Universalists at the ontic level hold that human rights exist for all peoples. Non-universalists at the ontic level hold that certain rights exist for only certain peoples at some times in particular cultures. A universalist at the epistemic level would say that all persons can know what their rights are, and a non-universalist at the epistemic level would say that not all persons can know such things.

Barbara: OK. So, a universalist might say that all persons have human rights. But then they would need to ask themselves whether having rights is inherent or intrinsic to being a human being.

Nina: Exactly. A foundationalist would add, not only do all persons happen to have human rights, but also that having those rights is inherent or intrinsic to their being human beings at all. That would be foundational.

Barbara: I guess, if you were a non-foundationalist, you would say that having rights is not inherent. If you had human rights, you'd have them as a matter of happenstance or contingency rather than necessity. They would be an achievement rather than a discovery—even if they were universal.

Nina: That's the point.

Barbara: Say again, Nina, with a specific example, what's the relation between realism, universalism, and foundationalism in regard to human rights?

Nina: A realist doesn't also have to be a universalist. A realist who is not also a universalist might say that some people in higher castes, such as Brahmins, have frame-independent rights, such as freedom of speech, the right to an education, or protection by the police. But untouchables, or "dalits" as they are known, don't. The claim that Brahmins have those rights is realist but not universalist. It would be a claim about a fact of the matter, but not a universal fact of the matter. Dalits don't have those rights. So, realism does not entail universalism.

Barbara: So now, couldn't a foundationalist add that Brahmins inherently have rights, and that untouchables inherently have no rights?

Nina: You're correct. The point about foundationalism is inherence.

Barbara: OK. I suppose you could be a realist but not universalist and not foundationalist about rights. You could suppose that it is a fact of the matter that Brahmins have the right to education, say, and that it is a fact of the matter that dalits don't. You could suppose further that that's not based on any foundational claim of inherence.

Adam: Nina, do you think that a non-universalist who recognizes that not all peoples share the right to an education could still argue that education should be available to everyone, even if it's not presently available for everyone?

Nina: Yes. I do. Maybe there's room here for a distinction between two kinds of universalism. The first kind is one we have been talking about so far. Call it an existential universalism, where, say, certain rights do universally exist. That holds that all persons share a certain trait. They all have a right to an education, say. Here's another sense of universalism. Call it a regulative universalism. It says that we should aim toward making such a right universal—with the emphasis on the "making." It recognizes that not all persons might actually have the right to education. But it invites us to take on the project of making education a right. In that way we can distinguish universalism as an existential claim, from universalism as a regulative ideal. In that way, an existential non-universalist could be a regulative universalist.

Barbara: Run that by me again.

Nina: The existential universalist says that universal rights do exist. In contrast, the regulative universalist claim says that we should strive to make such rights universal.

Adam: OK. That's fine as far as it goes. But if such rights are not foundational, what could make universalism ideal to start with? Doesn't the very idea of a regulative ideal require foundationalism?

Ronnie: I don't see that it does. Non-foundationalists could still set ideals for themselves without assuming that those rights—universal at present or in the future—are inherent to being a person.

Barbara: So, can you be a universalist without being a realist?

Nina: Yes. A universalist—say an existential universalist—could say that all persons share some rights and at the same time say that the very idea of a person and the idea of rights are constructions—they are made, not found.

Adam: I don't understand how you could not be a realist about rights.

Nina: Again, take the United Nations' Declaration of Human Rights. A universalist, who is not a realist, could say that human rights are, or should be, a cultural achievement, an endowment, a covenant. The rights it asserts are made, not found.

Human Life

Barbara: How might non-realism and non-foundationalism apply to the case of human life itself?

Nina: You could postulate human life itself as the highest value. But, at the same time, you could allow that that is not inherently or intrinsically so—that it could be otherwise. You could say that that postulated highest value is itself a human achievement that people need always to fight to achieve. But it's not a given. It's a taken. It's a contingent condition to which we assign moral priority. At the same time, you might say that there are circumstances under which you wouldn't hold it to be the highest priority.

Adam: I believe that human life is inherently valuable, independent of any reference frames.

Ronnie: I agree that human life has supreme value, yet it is postulated as supreme within a reference frame.

Adam: But if it's only supreme within a reference frame, how can it be supreme? Putting it within a reference frame makes it contingent.

Ronnie: Valuing human life is, in itself, a human achievement. It's a cultural achievement. Priority of human life is postulated. It endows human being with the highest value.

Barbara: I see where you're going, Ronnie. This is like one of the cases where the idea of the human being, to start with, is an achievement of classification, which postulates what it is to be human or humanly alive.

Ronnie: Precisely. Valuing human life need not be a foundational fact of the matter. It could be basic in a frame-dependent way—where you postulated it as such within a frame. It's a frame-dependent postulation.

Adam: But if it's a frame-dependent postulation, different people could postulate different things. Postulations could change over time. All we need is serious disagreement about what one should postulate within a frame, and then there would be no secure ground for the value of human life. That's way too fluid for me. Your idea of postulation makes morality too insecure.

Barbara: I don't quite see that, Adam. I don't see why we can't just get on with our lives as we do, even if others have different postulated views about human beings. Let there be differences about how people assign their value priorities. When serious conflicts arise, resolution would need to be negotiated as far as possible.

Adam: That's just it, Barbara. Diversity of postulations is fine. Except when people tenaciously embrace opposing values, which each takes to be most basic. That's when people start killing each other.

Nina: There are no guarantees about negotiations. No absolutism—neither realism, universalism, nor foundationalism—can guarantee success in negotiating conflicts.

Adam: OK. Try another example. What about your freedom? Don't you take that as foundational?

Ronnie: I take my freedom as basic, but I can imagine situations in which I might favor a life of personal bondage over freedom, say, for the well being of my loved one, or for the life of my community.

Adam: But in that case, wouldn't you then be identifying your loved one or the life of your community as an inherent good?

Ronnie: I don't think so. To say that you value one thing over all else in a particular circumstance doesn't mean that you couldn't value something else over all else in another circumstance. Valuing one thing in a particular circumstance doesn't require that it be an inherent or intrinsic value, independent of any reference frame.

Adam: That invites anarchy. It leaves open the possibility of arbitrarily postulating whatever you want.

Barbara: I see why you say that, Adam. But it also leaves open the possibility of discussing whether it would be reasonable to adjust your postulations in different circumstances.

Ronnie: Right. So, replacing your freedom with the freedom of your loved one or community won't show that your loved one's freedom or your community's freedom is inherently valuable.

Adam: Of course it does. When wouldn't the freedom of a loved one or your community be an inherent value?

Ronnie: I imagine that the freedom of a loved one or community could be trumped by a still more general value.

Adam: Like what?

Ronnie: Like the survival of the species. Imagine that to preserve the survival of the species, you'd have to curtail the freedoms of your loved one or community.

Adam: That's interesting. But wouldn't that make the survival of the human species inherently valuable?

Nina: What about the survival of the planet, the solar system, and so on? You could go on and on. I don't see any particular end to it.

Barbara: Why must there be any inherent value? Why not just keep moving from one non-inherent condition to another, always in relation to your provisionally postulated most basic value—without, that is, saying that that most basic value is inherently so?

Adam: But without some foundational bedrock, I don't know that I could see myself as having value at all. I would be without purpose or direction. There would be no point to it all.

Barbara: But you could chart your own direction, your own purposes and interests in accord with your own provisionally postulated highest values. Having purpose or direction doesn't require inherence.

Adam: Still, I believe that human life is inherently valuable, not derivatively so.

Ronnie: I value human life above all else as well. But I don't need to say that I value it irrespective of reference frames. Human value is always within some reference frame, some point of view, some context.

Adam: As I said, I believe that human life is inherently valuable. That's my foundational and realist moral principle. I also believe that it's frame-independent. I don't understand this idea of postulating basic values. There's no need to postulate anything. It just is an inherent value, period. That's the moral fact of the matter.

Ronnie: While I value human life too, I have difficulty understanding the idea of inherence or intrinsicality. Life isn't a foundational thing—not because we don't treasure life, but because there is no foundational anything.

Adam: I sure as hell believe life is the most basic thing for me.

Ronnie: It's the most basic thing for me too—in the sense that you and I give greatest value to our lives. But that's at one level of description. Life itself operates at the level of human beings. Yet, at subatomic levels, the very idea of being alive doesn't apply, just as the idea of a table doesn't apply at the subatomic level. When we agree that life is basic for us, we mean for us as live human beings. We don't speak from the level of electrons in empty space. But since the very idea of a human being isn't inherent, the value of human beings can't be inherent either.

Nina: Wait a minute. I just realized something.

Ronnie: What is it?

Nina: We've all been assuming that an inherent value—such as the value of human life—can't be trumped by another inherent value—such as the survival of the planet. We've been assuming that a trumped value can't still be inherent. But that's not quite right.

Ronnie: Why not?

Nina: There are two issues here. One issue is whether inherent values exist. Ronnie, you think none exists. And you, Adam, think some do. The other issue is whether, if inherent values exist, there must be a unique one that trumps all others. Such a unique value could not itself be trumped.

Ronnie: I don't get it.

Nina: Couldn't there be several inherent values without any one of them trumping all others? Just because a value might be trumped doesn't mean that it still can't be inherent, does it?

Ronnie: So you mean that there could be several inherent values without any one of them being the unique overriding value?

Nina: I don't see why not. Couldn't foundationalists hold that the value of human life is inherent and the value of survival of the planet is inherent? Couldn't they do so even if, in a terrible situation, the survival of the planet would trump human life? Why couldn't the value of human life still be inherent?

Adam: I've been assuming that an inherent value is a unique overriding value. If there were more than one inherent value then you'd have the problem of adjudicating between them. And I don't know how you'd do that.

Nina: That's my point. If several values could be inherent, it would take more than a given value's being inherent to decide between values. Just being inherent wouldn't be enough.

Adam: Anyway, I do have another candidate for a possibly highest inherent value.

Nina: What's that?

Adam: To be happy.

Barbara: Even if you say that your highest value is to be happy, that doesn't tell us very much, because so many people have such different ideas about what being happy actually means, or means for them.

Some people believe that their greatest happiness is to be found in the self-sacrifice of their human form—such as those women who engage in sati, or members of al-Qaeda.

Religious Examples

Barbara: OK. Let's move on to other examples that might answer to varieties of absolutism. How might realism, universalism, and foundationalism apply in religious cases?

Nina: When thinking about absolutism, for many people, God comes to mind.

Barbara: I guess you mean God as understood in the Abrahamic traditions—the Jewish, Christian, and Muslim traditions.

Nina: Yes, God understood as a personal creator God.

Barbara: So how might realism, universalism, and foundationalism apply in those cases?

Nina: At the ontic level, realists hold that the existence and nature of God is frame-independent.

Barbara: What do realists claim at the epistemic level?

Nina: At the epistemic level, they hold that the existence and nature of God is knowable or can be revealed.

Barbara: What about non-realism?

Nina: At the ontic level, non-realists hold that God is frame-relative, perhaps a construction of some kind of narrative theology. At the epistemic level, non-realists say we can't have frame-independent knowledge of God's existence.

Barbara: What about universalism? How might it apply?

Nina: At the ontic level, religious universalists—let's call them that—hold that God exists for all peoples. At the epistemic level, universalists believe that all peoples can know God's existence and nature.

Barbara: What about non-universalism?

Nina: At the ontic level, non-universalists believe that God exists for some but not for all people. At the epistemic level, non-universalists believe that God is knowable to some but not to all people.

Barbara: What about foundationalism? How might it apply to God as understood in the Abrahamic traditions?

Nina: At the ontic level, religious foundationalists believe that the existence and nature of God is irreducible and unanalyzable. At the epistemic level, they hold that God is knowable and unanalyzable.

Barbara: So what about non-Abrahamic traditions such as Buddhism or Hinduism? How might realism, universalism, and foundationalism apply there?

Nina: Buddhists hold that all that exists is conventional all the way down. It's empty of inherent existence all the way down. Even the view that it's conventional all the way down is itself conventional. It makes no exemption for itself.

Barbara: But don't you think that—by saying it's conventional all the way down—they need to allow that, that, in itself, suggests something foundational, that "all the way down" betrays a kind of foundationalism?

Nina: I can understand why you say that, but I expect that Buddhists would reply that even their postulation of emptiness itself is empty of inherent existence. They are thoroughly non-foundational.

Barbara: So how would realism and universalism apply to Buddhism?

Nina: Insofar as they say that all is conventional all the way down, they would have to be non-realist. But they would be universalist insofar as the emptiness of inherent existence holds for all that exists and there are no barriers in anyone knowing that that is so.

Barbara: So then how might realism, universalism, and foundationalism apply to Hinduism?

Nina: Here's an interesting contrast between Buddhism and Hinduism. Hindus hold that it's conventional almost all the way down.

Barbara: What do you mean by almost?

Nina: I mean that they believe that, at the ultimate level of reality, there is the Atma, Oneness, the undifferentiated unity. All else is conventional. That, in our terms, is what makes them foundationalists. The Oneness, the undifferentiated unity is their starting—and ending—point for everything that exists. Ultimately, everything is that. The rest is relative or conventional. The rest is a show, a parade, a non-reality.

Barbara: So how might realism and universalism together apply there?

Nina: Insofar as Hindus hold that ultimately, independent of any reference frame, Atman exists, they are realists and foundationalists. In addition, insofar as they affirm that all that exists ultimately is Atman, and there are no barriers to anyone knowing that that is so, they are universalists.

Barbara: That's interesting. Hindus are foundational while Buddhists are non-foundational. Hindus are realist while Buddhists are non-realist. But they are both universalists.

Nina: Yes. That's it. Of course, I need to add that, just like there are many sects and schools within the Abrahamic traditions, there are many sects and schools within Buddhism and Hinduism. There may be intramural differences in those non-Abrahamic traditions too. So let's keep in mind that my brief characterizations are generalizations.

Ronnie: So, Nina, remind us yet again why you've gone through all these cognitive, moral, aesthetic, and now religious examples. It's easy to lose sight of the larger point.

Nina: All right. My overriding point is that the very idea of absolutism comes in different strands—realism, universalism, and foundationalism. Whatever problems we might have with any single one of those strands, just negating it—as a relativist might do— won't result in a logical contradiction. You might disagree with realism or non-realism. You might disagree with universalism or non-universalism. You might disagree with foundationalism or non-foundationalism. But none of them are self-contradictory.

Hard and Soft Absolutism and Relativism

Barbara: So now that we have distinguished between some varieties of absolutism and relativism, let's see how they might be combined to make hard and soft absolutism or hard and soft relativism.

Nina: I guess the hard kind of absolutist is one who embraces all three— realism, universalism, and foundationalism. Softer kinds of absolutism are ones that embrace some but not all of those varieties of absolutism.

Adam: That means that I embrace a hard absolutism. I embrace realism, universalism, and foundationalism.

Barbara: That seems to be pretty straightforward. But it's not clear to me what softer versions of absolutism might look like, where only one or two of its varieties might be negated.

Nina: Let's see. A realist doesn't have to be a universalist. You could be piecemeal about what you take to be frame-independent. You could say that realism applies to some domains and not to others. And a realist doesn't have to be a foundationalist. A realist could hold that what is frame-independent doesn't have to be inherent.

Barbara: OK. I get that.

Nina: In turn, a universalist doesn't have to be a realist. The trait that might be universally common doesn't have to be frame-independent. Neither does a universalist have to be a foundationalist. The trait that might be universally common doesn't have to be inherent.

Barbara: I get that too.

Nina: Finally, a foundationalist doesn't have to be a universalist. You could be piecemeal about what you take to be foundational or inherent. Some but not all things might be inherent.

Adam: I can see that you can have realism without universalism or foundationalism. I can see that you can have universalism without realism or foundationalism, and, I can see how you can have foundationalism without universalism. But I can't see how you can have foundationalism without realism! That's because inherence needs to be attached to a frame-independent existent. I am a foundationalist and I need some inherent frame-independent existents to be foundational about. Inherence makes no sense for something that is reference frame-dependent.

Nina: I think Adam is right. You can't have foundationalism without realism.

Barbara: Adam, you also said that you could be a universalist but reject foundationalism. You could hold that all peoples actually exhibit common traits, but hold that those traits are not inherent.

Adam: Yes, I think that universalism without foundationalism is a logical possibility. But I believe that only foundationalism can actually explain the fact of the universal commonality of characteristics that all peoples might share. We need foundationalism to explain commonality. Without foundationalism, the commonality of shared characteristics would be a hugely unlikely coincidence. It would be miraculous.

Ronnie: I wonder. What about the universal instantiation of music appreciation in all cultures? Does that really require a foundational assumption? Without such appreciation would we really say of a culture that it is not a fully constituted culture? I wonder.

Adam: I think so. Even universal appreciation of music needs to be foundational. Otherwise, again, its universality would be a hugely unlikely coincidence.

Nina: So, now, whatever combination of varieties of absolutism we might embrace, at least we can now ask which varieties are necessary for absolutism, even a soft absolutism.

Barbara: I'd say that realism looks like it's essential for absolutism. Whether you're a hard or soft absolutist depends upon whether you add universalism or foundationalism to it. It looks to me as if absolutism at least requires realism. That would be minimal.

Nina: A hard relativist position, on the other hand, will be non-realist, non-universalist, and non-foundationalist. A softer relativist could be non-realist but could be universalist. But as a non-realist, one could not be a foundationalist.

Barbara: It's interesting, isn't it? Softer absolutists just might deny universalism. On that score, they could agree with a hard relativist.

Ronnie: That's an interesting observation.

Barbara: OK, then. Just to summarize, whatever other reservations we may have about realism, universalism, or foundationalism, the negation of each of them is not self-contradictory. The negation of realism—that a frame-independent order of reality exists and that we can know it—is not self-contradictory. The negation of universalism—that there are existents for all peoples or that all peoples can come to know them—is not self-contradictory. Likewise, the negation of foundationalism—that a most basic unanalyzable constituent of what there is exists, or that the comprehension of such a condition can be captured by first principles incapable of further analysis—is not self-contradictory.

Adam: Fine. Yet, it's one thing to say that those negations are not self-contradictory. It's another thing to say that they are true.

Nina: Of course. But if we go so far as to ask whether those negations of absolutism are true, we would need to ask—all over again—in what sense of truth?

Barbara: Now, if our discussions are going to turn back upon themselves like that, maybe it's time to ask a different sort of question, such as what we want to gain from these discussions? Maybe we want something besides truth, maybe something beyond truth.

Ronnie: What might that be?

Nina: Let's talk about that tomorrow.

Adam: Good idea.

~

Beyond Relativism and Absolutism

Nina: Yesterday we left off our discussion with your question, Barbara, about what it is that we want to gain from these discussions. You suggested that maybe we want something beyond truth. That question interests me very much.

Barbara: Yes, I'd like to hear what you have to say about that too, Nina. But first I need to tell you that I'm not so sure any more that my efforts to reconcile Adam and Ronnie weren't premature.

Nina: What do you mean, Barbara?

Supposed Oppositions between Relativism and Absolutism

Barbara: You know, on our second day, I tried to reconcile Adam's absolutism with Ronnie's relativism. I suggested a relative absolutism and an absolute relativism. But Adam and Ronnie couldn't agree about those. Nina, yesterday, after you disambiguated the possible strands or meanings of Adam's absolutism and Ronnie's negations of them, I thought that maybe we found at least some common ground between them. But I'm getting this nagging feeling that maybe relativism and absolutism can't be reconciled—not because we haven't hit upon an effective way to overcome the opposition between them, but because there's no opposition between them to start with. I'm beginning to think that relativism and absolutism can't really disagree with each other after all.

Nina: What do you mean, Barbara?

Barbara: I mean that Adam and Ronnie don't seem to be playing on the same field.

Nina: I don't get it.

Barbara: Let's go back to the original problem of self-reference, putting aside for the time being the strands of absolutism and relativism that we have unwoven.

Nina: All right.

Barbara: Relativists say that relativism is true. To be consistent, they must say that relativism is relatively true. In turn, absolutists say that absolutism is true. To be consistent, in turn, they must say that absolutism is absolutely true.

Nina: Yes, that's clear.

Barbara: So understood, absolutism and relativism are not on the same playing field. I'm not sure they can really compete with each other.

Nina: Why not?

Barbara: Well, consider this. The statements "Absolutism is absolutely true" and "Relativism is relatively true" do not contradict. The relativist cannot say, "Relativism is true" in the same sense of truth that the absolutist deploys when he says, "Absolutism is true." Between them, the very idea of truth must be equivocal. Each begs the question of truth itself.

Nina: So you don't think they contradict each other?

Barbara: No. They can't contradict each other since it's not the same sense of truth that one asserts and the other denies. They are talking past each other! As far as I can tell, Ronnie and Adam are at a standoff. For Ronnie and Adam to have a genuine disagreement—and not just an apparent disagreement—the sense of truth that they use must be the same. But according to each of their views, they are committed to different meanings of truth. I don't see an easy way to reconcile them.

Nina: Now I get it. When either of them says that his view is true and the other's is false—and vice versa—the very meaning of truth and falsity change between them. Equivocation is inevitable. They are already committed to divergent views about what could count as an answer to the question, "Which is true—relativism or absolutism?" Relativists and absolutists have to understand the question differently to start with.

Barbara: Maybe that's why the debate between relativism and absolutism has been around for so long, and there still seems to be no general agreement about it. In any case, this is another reason why they might not be able to be reconciled.

Ronnie: Exactly. That point was apparent in the case of relative absolutism and absolute relativism. To say that there's a frame-independent fact of the matter and that our understanding of it is frame-dependent—that's relative absolutism—or to say that we postulate certain assumptions as most basic in an inquiry and that our knowledge is frame-dependent—that's absolute relativism—uses the terms relative and absolute differently. They shift their meanings. They're not playing on the same field. They can't compete, because the absolute relativist and the relative absolutist use different meanings of absolutism!

Adam: I agree. Relative absolutism and absolute relativism don't share the same notion of absolutism. Absolutism for the relative absolutist means frame-independent. Absolutism for the absolute relativist means postulated as most basic within a reference frame.

Argumentative Purposes

Barbara: So, absolutists and relativists are wedded to different argumentative standards. Neither can accept the argumentative standards of the other.

Nina: What do you mean?

Barbara: Absolutists presume that relativists must adopt their absolutist argumentative purposes, and then declare relativism to be refuted when relativists fail to satisfy them.

Nina: Right.

Barbara: But giving reasons or arguments can have different purposes.

Nina: What other purposes might there be for giving reasons, other than convincing someone of the truth or falsity of a belief?

Barbara: When relativists offer reasons to the absolutist, they need not try to convince the absolutist. Relativists may give reasons or arguments just to present their views in an orderly way to promote a better understanding of their view. Without aiming to convince another person to embrace their view, relativists might seek to share their rationale for embracing a view.

Nina: So, as far as Ronnie's relativism is concerned, it seems that Adam is still free to embrace his absolutism. Of course, this doesn't show that Adam is right to adopt his absolutism.

Barbara: I agree. It only shows that the reasons Ronnie might adduce to bring Adam over to his relativist side are impotent in the sense that they can't do the job Ronnie would need to convince Adam. Ronnie's relativist reasons can't really have any argumentative traction to bring Adam over to his side.

Adam: I don't think that telling somebody why you embrace a belief is much of a reason if you don't mean to convince another person to embrace that belief. Reasons are supposed to convince us of the truth of something.

Ronnie: Sometimes we do give reasons to convince someone of a belief. But other times we give reasons to share our understanding.

Adam: I just don't see why we should call what you call reasons, reasons at all.

Ronnie: Well, since relativists recognize that all knowledge is relative, the most that they can show is that the absolutist program might be implausible in the relativist's own lights. The absolutist program makes impossible demands and issues in empty promises. On the other hand, we relativists can't rise to the absolutists' challenge for a frame-independent argument against the absolutist. But that's fine with me because such absolutist demands are inappropriate. Absolutists challenge relativists to show that the absolutist is wrong according to absolutist standards. But they are too demanding. In fact, if I succeeded in showing the absolutist to be wrong according to some absolutist standards, I'd be contradicting myself.

Adam: I agree, Ronnie. If you're unable to come up with absolutist reasons, you can't show absolutism to be wrong. That's fine with me. I don't have to help you to avoid a contradiction if you do try to refute absolutism on absolutist grounds. The fact is that your relativist reasons just aren't strong enough to count as reasons. After all, reasons are supposed to show why a belief is true or false. They are not supposed to show why a belief is true or false within some reference frame. They are supposed to show why a belief is true or false, period.

Ronnie: I don't see why you, Adam, should foist your burden of proof on to us relativists. Why should I adopt a standard that is impossible to achieve? Why should your absolutist standard of reason be the standard for any reason to be a reason in the first place?

Adam: Ronnie, I see why what anyone would count as a compelling reason for relativism or absolutism is itself controversial between us. As you indicated, some would say that we are both begging the question by insisting that we should assume the standards that we do.

Barbara: But I'm somewhat hopeful that we might still reconcile relativism and absolutism.

Nina: I don't know about reconciliation. But I do know that, once we have made clear what we mean by absolutism—be it realism, universalism or foundationalism—we can be clear about what it means to negate one or all of them. At least then we could have a real confrontation and not talk past one another. As for reconciliation, perhaps we have found all the reconciliation we can hope for. An absolutist and a relativist—at least softer ones—can agree about some of the combinations of realism, universalism, and foundationalism. That's a lot.

Adam: So again the questions arise, "Which of those absolutist or relativist views is true?" "In what sense of truth?"

Nina: Also, if we can, instead, ask the question whether realism, universalism, or foundationalism is true, or which of their negations is true, we would also need to ask, "In what sense of truth?"

Barbara: But again, if our discussions turn back on to themselves like that, maybe it's time now to ask that other sort of related question. Do we want something besides truth, something beyond truth?

Ronnie: Right. That's the question we started with today.

Adam: What might that something be?

Nina: I have some thoughts about that.

Barbara: Let's hear.

Self-Realization

Nina: So far, we've been asking about the truth or falsity of the varieties of relativism or absolutism. That's been our aim. In that regard, I'm impressed with Ronnie's arguments against absolutism, but I don't embrace relativism. I'm also impressed with Adam's arguments against relativism, but I don't embrace absolutism.

Barbara: Do you also have another aim besides the truth of those views?

Nina: Yes, I also aim for self-realization. But it's not just another interest. The pursuit of self-realization actually affects our understanding of the pursuit of truth, including the truth about relativism and absolutism.

Barbara: I suppose there are different ideas about the idea of self-realization. You could realize yourself as an individual in the sense of realizing your individual capabilities, for example.

Nina: Not quite. The idea of self-realization that I have in mind is different from that.

Barbara: What is it, then?

Nina: It's quite simple, really. It's something we all seek. We all seek freedom from the suffering of old age and death. We all seek freedom from the anxieties associated with our mortality. Self-realization—realizing who we really are—alleviates us from the anxiety of our finitude. Who we really are is One, without limit. Who we really are is indivisible, infinite, eternal, and free. All of us are embodiments of the One.

Barbara: I'm not sure I grasp what you mean. And I don't yet see how it could affect our understanding of the pursuit of truth.

Nina: Take the Hindu mantra, "Thou Art That," or, its first person variant, "I am I." The mantra says that all individual beings—human and non-human—are manifestations of the One—the birthless, the deathless. That One manifests itself as many. But ultimately the many is the One.

Adam: When you say, "I am I," or "Thou Art That," do you mean that you and I really are the One, or do you mean that you and I are like the One?

Nina: No, I mean that you and I and all individual beings *are* the One.

Adam: So, does that mean that I, as the individual person, Adam, is not real—or at least not ultimately real?

Nina: You are real—but only relatively or conventionally real. Ultimately, only the One exists. It's like, you're real within the reference frame of individuals, like this table is real within the reference frame of middle-sized objects.

Barbara: Do I understand Vedantic Hinduism correctly—at least your understanding of it—that when you recite the mantra, you're not only asserting that individual selves are embodiments of the One. When repeated in meditation, say, it also functions as an enabling vehicle?

Nina: Yes. It's both assertive and transformative. It helps us understand who we ultimately are. In turn, coming to realize that we are intrinsically the One, liberates us from the afflictions suffered from perceiving ourselves as individual selves. Final realization, call it enlightenment, brings refuge to the individual who suffers from falsely believing in his own mortality.

Barbara: You know, Nina, I don't often get anxious about my mortality. I just don't think about it that much.

Nina: Judging from my older and sometimes ill family members and friends, I expect that, as we get a little older, we will. But it's not just about death itself. It's also about the anxiety connected with limited time. I mean, sometimes I get anxious about not being able to do all the things I want to do—which, admittedly, couldn't be possible to do in one human lifetime. So I often tell myself that I'd better not waste any time. I'd better hurry up and do, and do, and do more. I drive myself crazy with that sense of impatience with everything that I do, since I need to get on with the next thing.

Barbara: So you think that the Hindu vision can help with that?

Nina: Most definitely. When I realize who I really am, when I put myself in the space of Oneness, in the space of silence, all of that frenzy goes away. I want to cultivate that habit of mind, or I should say, that habit of "no mind."

Ronnie: Say more about this space of Oneness.

Nina: OK. In the final realization, no subject-object duality exists, no self-other duality exists, no duality at all exists. The individual self is a manifestation of that Supreme Self, the Absolute Self, the Atman. The Absolute Self is undifferentiated unity—infinite, indivisible, pure, free, eternal. The One is not a number in contrast with two or any other number. It's beyond numerality. It's beyond expression. Repeating the mantra aids my coming to recognize that I am the One.

Ronnie: So, following your Hindu vision, you understand self-realization to be a process in which an individual self comes to know that he or she is the Supreme Self, a process in which the relative individual self comes to experience itself as the One, the Supreme Self. Is that it?

Nina: Yes. An individual's true nature is infinite and eternal. Insofar as an individual self is a manifestation of the Supreme Self, the individual self was never born and will never die. It is immortal. In the space of Oneness, in that space of silence, there is no duality, no argumentation, no assertion, no denial.

Ronnie: How does the realization that an individual self is a manifestation of the Supreme Self relate to meditation?

Nina: Repeating the mantra and focusing on it clears your mind and allows you to experience undifferentiated Oneness without thinking, without doing, without desiring. That leads to enlightenment. It is a space without attachment.

Adam: I don't share the aim you have, Nina. I, for one, am most interested in the truth—truth in contrast to falsity. That's a duality. I'm not so interested in a self-realization which, if you're right, leads to no duality.

Ronnie: I'm not so interested in your aim either, Nina. Even if Adam's and my understanding of truth differ, both of them are dualistic.

Barbara: Finally, we have something upon which you both agree! Maybe that's progress.

Self-Realization and the Relativism-Absolutism Debate

Barbara: So, Nina, if there's any relationship between the idea of self-realization and the debate between relativism and absolutism, what is it?

Nina: The relativism versus absolutism debate takes place in a particular level of consciousness, a level concerned with belief. Call it a relative level of consciousness. However, at a realized level of consciousness, the debate drops out. It ceases to be relevant.

Barbara: Are you suggesting that the relativism versus absolutism debate itself operates at a relative level of consciousness? Are you suggesting that sometimes you might be interested in leaving it behind? Is that it?

Nina: Yes. But leaving it behind is not the same as just changing the subject. It's not like saying that we've had enough of the debate about relativism and absolutism and now we're going to ask an unrelated question such as whether you prefer Indian food to Chinese food. Rather, I think that the debate between relativists and absolutists takes on a different character when you understand the larger space in which the debate is taking place. The debate between relativists and absolutists—which is a debate about which you should believe—looks quite different when you understand the larger space of non-belief, the space of Oneness, in which the debate is taking place.

Adam: I don't understand this idea of levels of consciousness or spaces of belief or non-belief.

Nina: Look at it this way. On the one hand, inquirers, who aim to explain a state of affairs, play a different role from seekers who aim to realize themselves. Yet these roles of inquirer and seeker are related. When inquirers utter the mantra, "Thou Art That," or "I am I," they aim to explain or elucidate a presumed state of affairs. In contrast, when seekers meditate on the mantra, they aim for something different from explanation or elucidation. But those roles are related. In the first instance, we may take the mantra as an assertion about the ultimate nature of things. In the second instance, we may take it as a vehicle for selftransformation. At some stage, though, the explaining becomes self-defeating. At that stage, talking undermines the achievement of the promised realization.

Barbara: I would think that there's an important connection between explanation and transformation. I mean, seekers could pursue the transformational aim only if—when they regard the mantra as an assertion or an explanation—they don't believe it to be false.

Adam: OK. If we actually believed that "Thou Art That" or "I am I" is false, then we couldn't very well pursue the self-realizational aim. I see that. But, you know, I might not believe that the kind of realization that Nina has in mind is false. That doesn't mean that I believe it's true either. I mean, for all I know, it's just incoherent. Nina, when you say, "I am I" in your special sense, I just don't get it.

Barbara: Adam, you're being hasty to think that if an utterance is neither true nor false it must be incoherent. It could be a poetic utterance. It could be a vehicle to put you in a certain state of receptivity.

Adam: I could take a pill to put me into a certain state of receptivity too.

Nina: Be that as it may, if we actually believed that, when we take "Thou Art That" or "I am I" as an assertion and regard it as false, we couldn't very well invoke it to aid in the self-realizational process. You would need to hold that the mantra is true—or at least assume that it's true—to receive its transformational benefit. At the same time, when you do assume it's true, you'd be operating in a relative space, a space of belief. Later in the process or journey, though, for the seeker, the question of its truth or falsity doesn't arise anymore. That question would inhibit the self-realizational process that the seeker is primarily interested in pursuing. The discussion of the possible truth or falsity of the mantra would short-circuit the realizational process. After some point, you can realize the One only if you transcend the intellectual discussion. You'd need to let it go.

Ronnie: I don't see how the positing of an undifferentiated Oneness, the "That" of the mantra, could explain anything. If your understanding is correct, Nina, the Oneness is beyond all dualisms. It's inexpressible. What kind of explanation could that be?

Nina: Well, as I said, it's explanatory at a preliminary stage of realization. At that stage, we're concerned with explanation. We're concerned with definitions, assertions, debates, and so on. It tells us something about the nature of what ultimate reality is. That is the level at which our discussions about relativism and absolutism have been going on between us. Yet, getting on with the project of realization requires our letting go of explanation. Ultimately, at the end of the process of realization, explanation drops out.

Barbara: Oh. So I hear you saying that different phases unfold one after the other. At one phase, the mantra might be explanatory. At another phase, it might be transformative. One iteration follows the next, so the nature of the mantra changes. Call it an iterative process. Is that a fair statement of what you're trying to convey?

Nina: That's it. I like that word, iterative. We pursue the debate within a space of dualism. That dualistic space is set against a background of a non-dualistic space, in which no distinctions exist, including the distinction between relativism and absolutism.

Ronnie: So you're talking about a space that backgrounds reference frames too, aren't you?

Nina: Yes. It's fine for you, Ronnie, to say that what there is and what we know of it are frame-relative. But I believe all reference frames reside within a larger space, a non-dualistic space. That space is called Oneness. Oneness is the space in which reference frames exist.

Adam: I agree that reference frames might exist within a larger absolute space. But I don't understand this idea of a non-dualistic space. For me, the space beyond reference frames is a space in which facts of the matter, absolute individuated facts of the matter, exist.

Nina: I agree with Ronnie that individuation is a construction of reference frames. But that doesn't mean that beyond reference frames there is nothing. What there *is* is the undifferentiated Oneness!

Ronnie: So, according to you, Nina, since Oneness is beyond all dualisms, the distinction between inherent and non-inherent couldn't apply there either. Is that it?

Nina: Correct. Oneness is neither inherent nor non-inherent. It is neither absolute nor relative. Oneness cannot be contrasted with anything else. Oneness alone is.

Ronnie: How can that be? In fact, you have distinguished Oneness from the relative human field. You can't have it both ways.

Nina: It depends upon your level of consciousness. It depends upon the point from which you're looking. If you speak from the Oneness, there are no distinctions. If you speak from the relative human space, there are. But even to speak of Oneness falsifies it, since doing so misleadingly suggests that Oneness contrasts with something else, namely the relative conventional field.

Dissolution of Distinctions

Barbara: So, Nina, what is the relation between Oneness and the relative field? Can you explain that?

Nina: The way you put it, Barbara, that question just doesn't arise.

Barbara: What do you mean? It sounds like a perfectly good question to me.

Nina: But look at the question. It really asks, "What is the relation between Oneness that has no relations and the relative that has relations?" To answer it at all—in any way—is to deny that that which has no relations, itself has no relations. Any answer would presuppose that that which has no relations has relations after all, since you've asked what is the "relation" between it and the relative field.

Barbara: I still don't get it.

Nina: OK. Look at it this way. Your question reduces to the question, "What is the relation of Oneness—the realm of no relations—to the realm of differentiated, countable individuals and their relations?" By just asking that question, you're rejecting the idea that there could be a realm of no relations. In the realm of no relations, there's no question of the relation between it and the realm of relations. Your very question disallows the realm of no relations.

Ronnie: I think we've uncovered a very interesting paradox here.

Nina: What is it?

Ronnie: When you invoke Oneness, you must invoke it from within a relative human reference frame. When you do that, you falsify the Oneness. The very distinction between the relative and the absolute frames appears within the relative frame. Yet, in the space of Oneness—that is, the unfalsified Oneness—there could be no distinctions. It's as if you need to start with the relative frame to set the ground for the movement toward the Oneness. Then, upon entry into the space of Oneness, all distinctions disappear, including the distinction that allowed you to enter into the space of Oneness to start with. It's like some kind of iterative logic, where one iteration leads to another, and the second undoes the first.

Nina: Yes, from the space of Oneness, there is no distinction between the Oneness and the relative realm. The very distinction between the relative and the Oneness does not exist. All that there ultimately is *is* the Oneness.

Barbara: But, as Ronnie just said, it's only from the relative field of the human that you can distinguish the relative human field from the Oneness.

Nina: I can concede that we draw the distinction between the relative and the absolute—between the human and the divine, if I may call it that—from within a relative field. But once in the space of Oneness—where the distinction between subject and object drops out, and where the distinction between the relative and the absolute Oneness drops out—any characterization of self-transformation must also drop out. The absolute, as articulated from within a relative reference frame, must be a falsification of it. For in the space of Oneness, no frames, no distinctions, no negations exist.

Barbara: That's why the distinction between the relative and the absolute is intelligible only from the reference frame of the relative. Speaking of the absolute from the relative reference frame falsifies it. We cannot speak of that which is beyond the relative. We must pass over it in silence. I guess that's what makes Nina's view a mystical view. This movement from the relative self to the posited absolute Supreme Self would involve a movement from a relative reference frame to a frameless absolute space.

Nina: I can agree that individual selves—limited to human systems of communication—can hope only very crudely to describe the ultimate Oneness. Oneness is ineffable. It is not describable. Any description falsifies the Oneness.

Barbara: I'm beginning to think of this like a ladder. It's like saying that to get to the higher place, to the place of Oneness, you need a ladder. But once you get to the Oneness, you will have kicked the ladder away.

Adam: I guess you mean that at a certain stage, what we experience is indescribable.

Nina: Correct. It's one thing to mentally grasp something. It's another thing to experience it. We can realize our Oneness, without being able to describe it.

Adam: Personally, I like the idea of not kicking the ladder away. I'd like to be able to retrace my steps, just in case I don't like where the ladder takes me.

Barbara: At least the ladder metaphor suggests, I think, that upon attaining Oneness, the relative field becomes dispensable. Here's another way to put it. Ronnie, you've been assuming that there's a distinction between relativism and absolutism.

Ronnie: Yes, I have. Adam and I both have.

Barbara: So, if the distinction between relative and absolute is, itself, relative, then your absolute, Adam, collapses into the relative. It depends upon the relative. So all that there is, is relative. That suggests that your idea of the absolute is, itself, not absolute. You get something like an absolute relativism that I suggested the day before yesterday.

Ronnie: Yes. That would be a situation in which you postulate the distinction between relative and absolute as most basic. But the postulation has to reside within a reference frame—a reference frame of human communicability, or the relative field.

Adam: You could, though, see the distinction between relative and absolute as generated from the space of the absolute. You could say that the distinction between relativism and absolutism recognizes some frame-independent features of the world. As it so happens, one of its frame-independent features is that an absolute frame-independent distinction between relativism and absolutism exists. In that case, the idea of absolutism takes precedence. Rather than the absolute collapsing into the relative—the relative is possible only by assuming the absolute.

Nina: Yet, even if the relative depended upon the absolute—or at least the absolute as "falsely" understood within the relative—the absolute Oneness has no need for any distinctions. It just *is*: pure. There's no need to confuse preparatory steps toward Oneness with Oneness itself. It only is what ultimately exists.

Barbara: Nina, it sounds like you think that Oneness is both relative and absolute, and neither relative nor absolute. It's both and neither. Am I right?

Nina: Precisely. It's both even though, to start with, that sounds like a contradiction. It's relative because it's in the relative field that the distinction between relativism and absolutism is drawn. It's absolute because, from the relative field, we may come to realize the absolute Oneness. That having been said, the absolute field where no distinctions are—including the distinction between relativism and absolutism, and, I might add, the distinction between knower and known—Oneness is unsayable. Of course, it's a paradox to *say* that Oneness is unsayable.

Ronnie: But even though you think of the absolute Oneness as separate from the relative field, it's not. It's in relation to the relative field that you think of the Oneness without another. As I understand it, it's from the relative field that the seeker strives for the absolute Oneness. You don't have an unrelated self-sustaining absolutism. The space of non-relations turns out to be a space with relations! So how does this compare with your absolutism, Adam?

Adam: My absolutism is completely independent of all reference frames. Nina's turns out to be dependent upon reference frames.

As well, my absolutism is describable. Nina's absolute Oneness isn't describable.

Nina: No, Adam. You're confusing the ladder with where the ladder might take us. While on the ladder, we may talk in terms of absolutism and relativism. But the ladder brings us to a place where neither relativism nor absolutism can be spoken. It is a place of silence. So now you see my dilemma. But it's a dilemma only from the reference frame of the relative field. But that is the reference frame in which we unavoidably are when we do speak at all. I cannot actually describe the Oneness, although I attempt to point to it somehow. Yet my pointing cannot succeed. I say that the Oneness is absolute, understanding that the very idea of the absolute contrasts with the idea of the relative. So, whatever I say in my attempt to describe the absolute—let me say, in its fully effulgent sense—must fail. In that way, when I speak of the absolute, it is relative and absolute and neither, because that to which I point—the fully effulgent absolute—cannot be successfully described.

Barbara: Nina, you've said that what there ultimately is, is relative and absolute, but neither relative nor absolute. How can that be?

Nina: Let's break it down. You're right that what there is is both relative and absolute. The relative field is the field in which you, Barbara, as an individual human being, have tea and cookies. The absolute field is that in which you as Oneness do not eat or drink. You are the space of Oneness, and such space does not eat or drink. So, yes, what there is includes both the relative and absolute fields.

Barbara: But I also recognize that even drawing the distinction—as a distinction at all—resides in the relative field. The distinction itself is a false distinction because it is drawn within the relative field.

Nina: Correct. That's because the relative field ultimately does not exist. Oneness alone is. That means that ultimately the relative field does not exist. You are right. I did start by distinguishing between the relative field and the absolute field. But that was only preliminary. They need to be transcended. Ultimately both fields—as distinguished fields—need to be negated. Of course,

when they are transcended, we could not articulate that we had.
We must remain silent.

Negation

Ronnie: So the absolute Oneness is a postulation within the relative field
of the sayable. Oneness itself is absolute—within a frame. All
reduces to postulation in a frame. From the relative, we postulate
the absolute. It's relativism because it's said. At the relative level,
Oneness is best understood within the terms of absolute relativism, as Barbara has outlined.

Nina: Correct. But while we postulate the distinction between relative
and absolute, we go on to negate it.

Barbara: You affirm the absolute. Then you recognize that having done
so implicates a distinction involving a contrast with the relative. You see that that distinction itself is false. So then you negate the absolute as a contrast with the relative. In other words,
you affirm the Oneness that is beyond the absolute *and* the relative, all the while conceding that any such affirmation—insofar
as it is said—remains at the relative level. *Then* you negate the
relative. *Finally*, you accept what alone *is*, namely, the Absolute
Oneness.

Nina: Yes. I say that Oneness is neither relative nor absolute. That is so
because to say that a relative field ultimately exists is false. Also,
to say that what there ultimately is, is absolute, is also false—because I am *saying* these things at all. All that I say is false because
I am *saying* them. What there is, ultimately, is neither relative
nor absolute, because ultimately, there is neither relative nor
absolute. Oneness is neither relative nor absolute.

Barbara: But here's what puzzles me about all of that.

Nina: What is it?

Barbara: You're talking about negating dualisms. What about negation
itself?

Nina: Negation itself, as you rightly anticipate, Barbara, is something we do. We negate. What we do is in the relative field.

Barbara: So ultimately, negation does not exist.

Nina: Correct.

Barbara: So when we first affirm that what there is, is both the relative field and the absolute field, and then negate that what there is, is both the relative field and the absolute field, we are doing something— that is, negating. But ultimately, negation does not exist.

Nina: Correct. Negation exists and does not exist.

Barbara: Some people would say that's a contradiction.

Nina: Contradiction exists only in the relative field. But the relative field does not ultimately exist. In Oneness, we are no longer in the space of logic.

Ronnie: Wow. That really does worry me. Specifically, what I'm worried about is the "not." The negation. In other words, if you say that Oneness just is, that it's neither relative nor absolute, you've used a negation: *not* relativism and *not* absolutism.

Nina: So?

Ronnie: So, by introducing the negation, you have re-introduced a duality. Negation contrasts with affirmation. No contrasts with yes.

Nina: What about this? Why not say that, when confronted with the distinction between the relative in contrast with the absolute, we should just put it aside?

Ronnie: But now, "putting aside" negates "not putting aside." We wouldn't be any further, would we?

Nina: When I say negate all dualities, that also applies to negation. You eventually drop negation too. Then you are in the state of "no thought." Your thinking gets short-circuited. It's a state of bliss.

Barbara: Now I'm beginning to see how this all connects with your ultimate aim of realization. It's happiness. It's freedom from our worries of mortality and from the anxieties caused by our minds. It's bliss.

Nina: Yes.

Adam: Nina, you call it a state of bliss. It sounds to me more like a state of blankness. Nothingness. What's blissful about that? What guarantees are there that it's a state of bliss?

Nina: For you to accept its blissfulness you would need to experience it. You would need to try it.

Barbara: I guess I'm having some trouble letting go of the relative field and yielding to Oneness, about which we can't speak without falsifying. Yet Nina, you do speak about it, even if in doing so you falsify it.

Nina: When speaking about it, we can use different words: Oneness, Supreme Self, Knowingness, Bliss, Love, and so on. That's not because any of these words is right or wrong. The best we can do is to use different words and metaphors without getting stuck on any one of them. It's a preliminary way of talking. Even to say, "I am I," you will falsify. But doing so, in a preliminary way in the iterative process, will help you to shift the subject from an individual "I"—Barbara—to Oneness. Once you do that, you will surrender to the realization of Oneness.

Barbara: I can see, maybe in the abstract, how that just might lessen my anxieties about loneliness, bodily illness, or death.

Adam: OK. Let's grant that that might happen as a consequence. Maybe that's an individual matter. But isn't this a bit of philosophical overkill?

Nina: What do you mean, Adam?

Adam: Well, maybe some talk therapy about the anxiety of loneliness, illness, and death might help without importing all of this mysticism about a reality that's inexpressible, about surrender, and all of that? As I said before, maybe pills would be enough without this ineffabilist ontology, this mysticism.

Nina: It's more than a short-term fix for a passing anxiety. Who we really are was never born, and will never die. In Oneness, the very idea of mortality does not apply.

Adam: You know, Nina, the more I hear you, the more I get the sense that the movement from the individual self to the divine Oneness, to the Supreme Self involves a kind of blasphemy. Your individual self assumes or appropriates the place of the Supreme Self. That's presumptuous, to say the least.

Nina: But Adam, you have it the wrong way around. For persons to *deny* that their true individual selves are the Supreme Self would be blasphemous. Such denial would actually demean the individual selves, for they are manifestations of the One. For, they are "That."

Ronnie: Nina, I'm puzzled by the underlying motivation of your transformational journey. You say that the goal of human life is that we should have perfect happiness, bliss with no pain or suffering, and no division of any kind. You claim to know what human beings want. You claim that death does not apply to individual selves, because the individual self, which would otherwise be thought to die, is a manifestation of the eternal One. One's true nature is beyond the relative self. So, one possible motivation for embracing your kind of realizational program is to avoid anxiety about loneliness, illness, and death.

Nina: Yes.

Ronnie: Now, whatever else may survive after my bodily death, I surmise that I lose my individuality. It's that that I'm anxious about. As a human being, I don't care that something beyond my individuality might be eternal.

Nina: But it's as a human being who is anxious about your bodily death and the cessation of your individuality, as you say, that your realization of who you really are will help. The realization will alleviate your human suffering.

Displacing the Human Self

Barbara: Wait a minute. It's easy to think of who I am as the individual human person called Barbara, in contrast with you—the individual human person called Nina.

Nina: Yes. That takes place at the relative human level. But if I transcend the human level, that is, transcend the duality between us, I will negate the duality between us, between all individuals. Then it's no longer Barbara, or Nina, Adam, or Ronnie. It's all One.

Barbara: So then you deny individuality. Individuality turns out to be merely relative. It operates at the relative, conventional, or the human level. Is that it?

Nina: Yes.

Ronnie: My point is that your identification of the individual human self with the Supreme Self, with Oneness, displaces the human self.

Nina: What do you mean?

Ronnie: Well, for example, as human beings, we often ask ourselves, "How am I doing?" "Am I getting ahead with what I need and want?" "Should I take on one project or another?"

Nina: Yes. So?

Ronnie: Well, those sorts of questions are swept aside by identifying my individual self with the Supreme Self, with Oneness.

Nina: I'm not saying that the individual self doesn't exist. It does, but at a secondary or relative level. Still, by focusing on those sorts of questions, you distance your individual human self from your true Self.

Ronnie: But sometimes it's important to concentrate on the human self. For example, my human self needs food and shelter. It wants companionship and love. It wants to live with a measure of security and comfort, and so on. For this, you have to engage in all kinds of human activities.

Nina: Yes. We need to be mindful of that. Sometimes we, as individuals, need to become part of the parade, you might say, and that's all right if, when we do, we realize it's just a parade.

Ronnie: But the displacement of the individual self does away with—or at least minimizes—lots of questions of well-being.

Nina: Keep in mind that realizing Oneness consoles personal suffering and loss. The pursuit of Oneness actually facilitates human well-being.

Alleviating Suffering

Barbara: I can see how embracing the idea that who we really are is the One just might alleviate suffering, particularly anxieties about loneliness, illness, or death. Even though we may have family and friends, in the end, each one of us is really alone—alone, I mean, as individuals. Even when family and friends surround us, within our selves, we're always alone.

Nina: So you agree with me that the idea of Oneness might help with that?

Barbara: I can see how it might. But it comes at a high price.

Nina: What's that?

Barbara: Well, if you say, it's OK, you're really not alone—not because you really have other individuals in your life, but because, as an individual, ultimately you don't really exist, that can't be much comfort. It's like saying you're mistaken to think that you could even be alone, because you're not even an individual. You never were! It's like saying it's a mistake to even think that who you are is capable of being alone. It's like saying that the very idea of aloneness does not apply to who you really are. It's the same for the anxieties about illness and death. You're wrong to be anxious about illness and death, because who you really are is without illness or death. It's a mistake to think that you can become ill and die. In Oneness there's no anxiety about anything.

Nina: So, what's the price?

Barbara: What's the price? It's obvious. Again, it's the price of your individuality. That's what you lose.

Nina: You can't lose what you never had. You don't lose anything. You never really were an individual. How could you lose it?

Barbara: You think it's a category mistake for me to say that I'm an individual. But it's as an individual human being that I know and value anything. If I lose my individual I—I mean the individual I that I am—I couldn't believe anything. I couldn't know anything. I couldn't value anything.

Nina: You are an individual—but only at the relative level. Who you ultimately are is One. You as an individual can believe or know or value things of a dualistic kind. Yet such kinds of knowledge and values are secondary or mundane.

A Broken Promise

Barbara: Nina, here's a related worry I have about your motivation to avoid human anxieties about loneliness, illness, and death.

Nina: What is it?

Barbara: If you become realized—if the promise of the realization were fulfilled—then no individual self would exist anymore to be satisfied. There would no longer be an individual self to whom the promise of realization was initially made!

Adam: Right! If the movement from the individual self to the Oneness abrogates the individual self, then upon realization, no individual self would be left to be relieved of any of the anxiety.

Nina: In a way, you're right. What the individual self had first desired would no longer matter. In Oneness, the question whether the individual self had succeeded in getting what it wanted would no longer arise. It would have become irrelevant.

Barbara: So, starting out on the path toward realization, the individual self couldn't really say what the destination would really be like. It really couldn't fathom where such a self would go. Then, upon arrival, the individual couldn't say that the individual had successfully arrived because it would no longer be the individual that could arrive anywhere at all. So the question whether the original intention to be realized had actually been satisfied is unanswerable.

Adam: I would surely want to know if, at the end of the program, I had succeeded or failed.

Ronnie: Yes, the would-be promise of realization made to the individual self would have been undone when the individual self would have been realized. Promises to the individual self would no longer apply. The initial individual self would no longer be there to "accept" or to "experience" any promised fulfillment.

Barbara: So, I guess ironically, whatever consolation the program of transformation might have promised, it couldn't console the individual self that originally wanted to be consoled. Of course, the individual self, to whom the promise of consolation would have been made, would no longer need consolation. The notion of need would no longer apply.

Ronnie: Exactly. In the movement from individual self to Supreme Self, the individual self would no longer be there to be consoled. So, with the realization of the Supreme Self, the initial motivating aim of realization would drop out too.

Barbara: To my way of thinking, the individual self apparently can't be satisfied with its own transformation. It seems as if the realization of the individual self entails its own abrogation.

Nina: You are right. The very idea of satisfaction of an individual self would no longer apply.

Intentionality

Ronnie: Here's a further worry I have about the individual self being abrogated. I'm wondering whether you have to be an individual to know anything at all. I mean, if I know that the sun will rise over the Ganges tomorrow, I have to believe it. Only as an individual person can I believe anything at all. So if I—as an individual person—don't exist, how can I know anything?

Nina: You as an individual person can know such things. But such individual knowledge is mundane compared to the pure Awareness of who you really are.

Ronnie: Well, now I wonder, when one is realized, what objects of knowledge can exist. I mean knowing, for example, is like being conscious, or thinking, imagining, experiencing, hoping, and desiring. A person can't be conscious without being conscious of something. We can't think without thinking of something. Individuals can't imagine without imagining something. We can't experience without experiencing something. We can't hope without hoping for something. We can't desire without desiring something. Those are so-called intentional attitudes. So, Nina, how can anyone know the Oneness which resists all dualisms?

Nina: You're correct. Where no distinction between knower and known exists, no knowledge in its mundane relative human sense can exist, for such knowledge is inherently dualistic. In the state of realization, knowledge in the mundane, relative, human sense can't apply. Individual selves cannot experience without experiencing something. So in the fully realized state— where the distinction between experiencer and experienced doesn't apply—"experience," in its mundane, human sense, can take no object.

Adam: So I guess no individual person could really experience One-ness, since in such a state, you couldn't really experience any-thing at all.

Nina: That's correct if you mean that in such a state you couldn't ex-perience anything as understood in its mundane, relative, human sense. But what's important is that you could have or be pure knowingness, pure awareness, pure consciousness—where there are no objects of knowing, no objects of consciousness, no objects of awareness. Awareness just is.

Barbara: So then what about the distinction between relative, mundane knowledge and so-called pure Knowingness, or pure Awareness, or pure Consciousness?

Nina: As I say, such pure attitudes take no object whatever. They are very different from what we usually call their mundane cousins—awareness *of*, consciousness *of*, and so on. Perhaps to call them by such similar names as Awareness or Consciousness is misleading. Perhaps so. Having said that, though, Oneness is pure Awareness.

Adam: Nina, you say that Oneness is pure Awareness. But still, aware-ness does have to take an object. When you are aware, you are aware of something. It's inherently dualistic. It doesn't matter that you've inserted the word "pure" before it. Your inserting the word pure doesn't make it non-dualistic.

Nina: I mean something else by pure awareness than what our language allows. But our language is all that I have to communicate with when I speak with you. So in one sense, you're correct. The phrase "pure awareness" is a falsification of what I am pointing to. I just mean to use language to point to something that can't be stated. Unlike you, I don't take the limits of language to be the limits of knowledge or the limits of awareness.

Adam: But even if awareness, in your special sense, were to take no ob-ject, if it were not dualistic—and I don't quite get how it could not be—it's a pretty big leap to say that who we are is that pure Awareness—or, as you also say, that who we are is the pure, the free, the eternal. That's a pretty big leap.

Nina: There is no leap. Only that is what ultimately exists. All individuals can only be That. There's no question of the relation between who you are and what that is. There is only that—Oneness. I admit, though, that saying so falsifies the nature of Oneness.

Ronnie: But Nina, if what you say is a falsification, why should we listen to what you say? Why should we take it seriously?

Nina: It's your choice. I have conceded that my tools of expression are self-defeating. But you may look beyond them to a deeper reality I am trying to convey.

Ronnie: But how can I choose between two alternatives, one of which is clearer and more familiar, and the other, which is so mysterious that I can hardly make sense of it? As far as I can make out, the limits of the sayable are the limits of knowledge!

Nina: Ronnie, how do you know that?

Ronnie: I guess I don't know that. But anyway, I don't really need to make a judgment about it. I have plenty to deal with in the space of the sayable.

Barbara: Nina, you have actually said quite a lot about realization and Oneness in relation to absolutism and relativism. So, even though our language might be defective, as you say, I'd still like to revisit a couple things about what you have said.

Nina: By all means.

Barbara: Well, suppose—just suppose—that we made a serious practice of meditating on "Thou Art That," and that resulted in alleviating our anxieties about loneliness, old age, or death.

Nina: Yes. That's what I have been urging.

Barbara: That would be a good thing. But even if it had that result, that wouldn't necessarily show that the benefits of meditation depend upon overcoming any dualism of language. It wouldn't show that all that ultimately exists is the inexpressible Oneness. It wouldn't show that the Oneness is pure, free, or forever. In other words, the benefits of meditation wouldn't depend upon the ontological claims that you say go with it. It wouldn't show that those ontological claims are true—in whatever sense of truth you care to embrace. Couldn't I just get on with meditating and see if it works, without having to first conclude that the ontological assumptions you make are true?

Nina: Yes, of course you could. But if they have the desired effect, then that would at least suggest, wouldn't it, that those assumptions are true?

Barbara: I don't know. It might work for reasons other than the truth of the ontology. I mean, to take a different example, we could embrace a religion because it might have a desirable effect like, say, consolidating a community. But even if it did that, it wouldn't show that that religion was true, much less intelligible. Having a desirable effect doesn't make something true, or intelligible.

Ronnie: That's right. I'm interested in truth. So, if you don't mind, Nina, can we go back to reconsider a couple of those ontological presuppositions?

Nina: Sure. But keep in mind, while I may not be able to convince you of their truth, if it were to work for you, that might be enough for you to take it seriously. I mean, many people go to medical doctors or to acupuncturists for ailments without being concerned about the truth of their presuppositions. They want to know if it works, or if it works for them.

The Sayable Revisited

Ronnie: Nina, I don't embrace your view about the inherent limits of language. I mean, to say that language falsifies Oneness, I'd have to be able to compare a frame-independent ultimate reality with a frame-dependent description. But I don't have access to the ultimate reality even to make the comparison. A relativist like me doesn't have to go that far. I could just withhold judgment about what might exist beyond reference frames.

Adam: I have to agree with Ronnie on that point. Nina, how do you know how ultimate reality is before language? How can you say that it is not describable? How do you know that the ultimate reality isn't already dualistic? How do you know that language is inadequate? How do you know all that?

Nina: I can know because we can have access to ultimate reality. We can acquaint ourselves with it through meditation, for example, when the veil of language is removed, when all dualisms drop out. Then we will realize our true Self.

Barbara: But we can't describe it. That's also your belief.

Nina: Yes, I believe all language falsifies the true nature of what there is. So insofar as both relativism and absolutism are in some language, they falsify the true nature of what there is.

Adam: So if I understand you, Nina, you believe that some fact of the matter exists independent of reference frame?

Nina: Yes. Our true nature, who we ultimately are, precedes all statements and all reference frames. Moreover, while we can know it, it is unsayable.

Adam: Surprisingly, that sounds remarkably similar to my absolutism, except I don't add that if we're not silent about it, we'd falsify it.

Nina: Adam, I can see why you say that I'm not that far from your absolutism. But I'm really not such a close ally as you might think.

Adam: Why is that?

Nina: Because your absolutism is a theory formulated within a language. Your absolutism is dualistic. My absolute goes beyond any theory of absolutism. It goes beyond any theory of relativism. For that matter it goes beyond any theory.

Barbara: I'm struck by the thought that Ronnie's relativism and Nina's mysticism can actually agree that any putative ultimate facts of the matter cannot be stated in human terms.

Ronnie: Yes, my relativism holds that truth, for example, is relative to a reference frame, and it remains silent about a putative undifferentiated Oneness beyond frames.

Nina: At the same time, Ronnie, I don't see that you can deny the existence of such a Oneness.

Ronnie: I don't deny it. I remain silent about it. I remain agnostic about it. It's just that it can't help us regarding knowledge—at least the kind of knowledge I'm concerned with.

Nina: Of course, Ronnie, your relativism is not my mysticism. My mysticism affirms that there is an ultimate realm, but we must remain silent about it. To that extent, my mysticism agrees with your relativism. Your relativism remains silent about what you say is only my putative frame-independent realm. My mysticism remains silent about it because language is inherently falsifying. Silence is appropriate for both of us, even if it's for very different reasons.

Adam: Well, my absolutism affirms that there is a fact of the matter, a frame-independent world. It's knowable, and I can talk about it.

Ronnie: At the same time, Adam, all of Nina's talk about realization operates at the relative level. Despite its being about Oneness, it can't be foundational. It's beyond the foundational. To speak of it as inherent, in contrast to non-inherent, is to falsify it.

Adam: So, Nina, tell us again why we should take on the project of realizing ourselves to start with?

Nina: Because it is in our nature to seek happiness and to avoid suffering. Enlightenment about who we really are will help us do so.

Adam: So it's in our relative human nature to realize ourselves.

Nina: Yes.

Adam: That sounds like a foundationalist answer! So, at the relative or the human level, you're an absolutist of a harder kind after all!

Nina: You might be tempted to say so. But, again, in the space of Oneness—where no distinctions exist—you cannot say so.

Adam: Nina, you say that human beings inherently seek to be happy, that is, without suffering. That's a foundationalist claim. But according to you, we eliminate suffering by realizing Oneness, which disallows foundationalism.

Ronnie: In that sense, Oneness is non-foundational, but at the relative level it is foundational.

Nina: Ultimately, there's no foundational or non-foundational, no realism or non-realism, no universalism or non-universalism, no absolute or non-absolute, no relative or non-relative.

Adam: But what kind of claim is that, an absolute or a relative claim?

Nina: Mysticism denies your relativism, Ronnie, and your absolutism, Adam. Speaking at the relative level, Oneness is not relative. It's beyond the relative. Speaking at the level of Oneness, it's not absolute. It's beyond the absolute. It's neither relative nor absolute. Yet, insofar as I speak at all, I speak at the relative level. At the relative level, Oneness is relative because it is spoken about. Yet still at the relative level, Oneness is absolute because it is frame-independent. Still speaking at the relative level, Oneness is both relative and absolute. At the same time, still speaking of Oneness at the relative level, Oneness is neither absolute nor relative.

Dissolution of the Debate

Barbara: Nina, you seem to think that the debate between Adam and Ronnie dissolves because language can't capture the way things are. You think that language is inherently limited because of its essentially dualistic nature. So, since both Adam and Ronnie's arguments—inevitably in a language—seek to capture how things are, they both must fail to do so.

Nina: Yes, that's pretty well it. The debate dissolves itself. It deconstructs itself. That's why I think we should move on and ask the deeper question, namely, what we really want. My answer is that we really want to eliminate or at least minimize our suffering as individual human beings.

Barbara: Of course, I want to minimize human suffering too. But I think your dismissal of the debate is too hasty.

Nina: Why?

Barbara: Even if you were right about language falsifying itself, that wouldn't show anything peculiar or distinctive about the debate between relativism and absolutism.

Nina: What do you mean? The fact that language falsifies itself shows that there is something deeply flawed about the debate between relativism and absolutism.

Barbara: That's just it. It would show too much.

Nina: Too much? How could it show too much?

Barbara: If your claim against the sensibility of this debate were right, it would also show that any debate—not just this one—would be pointless! It would show that any argument in favor of, or opposed to, any side of any debate would be pointless.

Nina: In a way, you're right, Barbara. Perhaps it's best to do away with all debates.

Barbara: Oh, my. That's not exactly the inference that I expected you would draw. So you really do want your argument to do that much. Actually, though, when I said your thesis of ineffability or unsayability does too much, I also meant that there's a sense in which it also does too little.

Nina: How could that be?

Barbara: Well, when you come to think of it, Nina, your thesis of ineffability—while it could apply to all discussions—might not be as drastic as you make out.

Nina: How could the thesis of ineffability not be so drastic, as you say?

Barbara: Consider this. Suppose I try to describe the smell of a rose or the taste of rhubarb. My description could only be very general, only approximate. All attempts to describe them perfectly would be frustrated. In the end, I'd have to invite you to actually smell or taste. No description in a language would do the trick. Now, you might be tempted to say that that's a failing of language, or a failing of a language at a particular stage of its development. You might be tempted to say that, given enough time, a language could be perfected in a way not to falsify at all.

Nina: I'm not sure that language could ever be so perfected as to be able to perfectly capture such smells or tastes. The fact that language falsifies seems inherent to language itself.

Barbara: I agree. The imperfection of language is inevitable.

Nina: So we agree that language systematically falsifies.

Barbara: Yes. But even so, that would not show that all argumentation and discussion were pointless. It would only show that we would have to accept language as approximate. And that might be good enough. There's no point in rejecting the good because it's not perfect!

Nina: You mean I've been too demanding of language? We can allow argumentation and discussion with language that's only approximate?

Barbara: Yes. I think so. I just don't see why you think that the disagreement between Ronnie's relativism and Adam's absolutism dissolves because language can't perfectly capture the way the world is. That's what I meant when I said that your ineffabilist argument might do too little to necessitate your conclusion.

Nina: I recognize, of course, that you're trying to poke a hole in what you think is my argument.

Barbara: Of course.

Nina: But that already presupposes that I should care about such holes.

Barbara: Yes, I think you should care about such holes, even if the language in which it is expressed is approximate. It's good enough to be taken seriously. I hope you will.

Nina: It has its place. But I think its place is more limited than what you, Adam, and Ronnie seem to think it is.

Meditation and Other Minds

Barbara: In any case, Nina, you know what? I am, nevertheless, much attracted to joining you on the meditative path. I would just be careful about presuming that it will lead to a special knowledge about a deeper reality.

Nina: It's your choice, Barbara. All I can say is that, if you will join me in meditation, you will experience things differently. You will discover that it yields a non-ordinary knowledge, a kind of enlightenment.

Barbara: Well, of course, I can't actually argue with that. Your promise rests on an invitation to experience certain things. Maybe after joining you on your meditative path, I can then examine what I have gained. But I anticipate that there will be an obstacle even after we share in our meditative path.

Nina: What's that?

Barbara: I keep thinking about our experience on the Ganges—not so much about the floating dead baby who shocked us on our first day though.

Nina: What was it then?

Barbara: I keep thinking about the Hindu sadhus and their devotees, who were meditating. In my walks along the Ganges these last few days, I noticed that it's not just the Hindus who were meditating. It was the Buddhist monks too. Western visitors like us were meditating as well. They were all pursuing meditative practices of one sort or another.

Nina: So what's puzzling about that?

Barbara: I keep wondering about what they were actually experiencing. I mean, you say that, after we embark on the meditative path, we can talk about that special knowledge we will have gained. But I keep thinking that whatever we will have experienced, we really can't know that we are experiencing the same thing as anybody else. If the Hindu saddhu or the Buddhist monk say that, through meditation, they have gained a special kind of knowledge about ultimate reality but, at the same time, if they don't agree with each other about its nature, what then? How can they know, or how can we know that they or we really are disagreeing with one another about a common experience? How would we know that when we meditate, we are experiencing the same thing?

Nina: What are you driving at?

Barbara: It's this. However beneficial meditation might be for each of us in different ways, I wonder whether we could really know whether what you will have experienced and what I will have experienced is the same, or whether it will have enabled us to grasp the ultimate reality. I wonder whether the Hindus, Buddhists, and visitors all might be in the same situation.

Nina: I guess I can't answer that question. We'd need to embark on the meditative path and after then maybe raise those questions.

Barbara: I look forward to that.

Nina: I do too. But you know what? Before, you said that there's a problem about my idea of the imperfection of language. You warned me not to reject the good because it's not perfect. I now think that your new problem about not being able to tell if our experiences in meditation agree with each other is a bit like that. You're wondering whether the difficulty we might have in knowing what other persons experience disallows communicating with them about it.

Barbara: What's your point, Nina?

Nina: Your worry about other minds might apply to anything that any two persons might experience—whether it's what we experience when meditating, or smelling roses, or tasting rhubarb, or anything else. Yet we still manage to share our experience—even if it's approximate, even if it's imprecise.

Barbara: I take your point, Nina.

Nina: I'm glad, because you gave it to me first.

Self-Realization: Relativist or Absolute?

Barbara: So, there you have it, Adam and Ronnie. What do you—as individual human beings—think about what Nina has been saying?

Adam: I don't know what to say. I guess that's because, if I follow Nina, she'd say that anything I do say would automatically falsify itself and that would include anything I have to say about absolutism or relativism. What are your thoughts, Ronnie?

Ronnie: I feel the same way. I'm stymied. But you know, I think we're at a very interesting crossroads.

Barbara: What do you have in mind, Ronnie?

Ronnie: Well, when Adam argues for his absolutism, he argues for the rightness of his view. I'm doing the same thing when I argue for my relativism. Whatever differences might be between us, we're both in the same game. We're both arguing to get closer to the truth even though we disagree about what truth itself is. We're in the same general ballpark. But Nina isn't. She's interested in eliminating suffering, which she thinks is caused by the dualistic sorts of activities that Adam and I are pursuing.

Adam: Yes, Ronnie, I think you put it very well. That pretty well captures my frustration. Rational thought involves subject-object dualities. It involves distinguishing between what a thing is from what it is not. It involves assertions of truth or falsity, reasonableness and unreasonableness, and so on. So if we overcome all dualities, rational thought drops out too.

Barbara: Still, how does Nina's view of Oneness fit with relativism or absolutism, allowing, of course, that we're talking about it? Is she a hard absolutist? Does she embrace realism, universalism, or foundationalism? Or is she a relativist who negates realism, universalism, or foundationalism?

Adam: I think it's clear. As Nina sets it out, her view of Oneness is absolutist insofar as it is realist, universal, and foundational. She weaves together all three strands of absolutism. It's realist because Oneness exists independent of any reference frame. It's universal because she thinks all persons seek their own realization. Finally, it's foundational in that all persons inherently seek their own realization. It's in human nature to do so. Moreover, her view is foundational because Oneness is inherent, irreducible, unanalyzable, and inexpressible. Put them together and that makes Nina a hard absolutist.

Barbara: I understand why you say that. But you know what? She's also not an absolutist at all.

Adam: Why is that?

Barbara: Because absolutism is a theory. So is relativism. Since theories are dualistic, and Nina is beyond dualism, she can be neither absolutist nor relativist. So paradoxically, she is both a hard absolutist and not absolutist at all.

Ronnie: We have to ask, though, from what reference frame is she absolutist, relativist, or neither? Is she absolutist from the field of the absolute? According to her idea of Oneness, she couldn't be either absolutist or non-absolutist. She couldn't be realist or non-realist, universalist or non-universalist, foundationalist or non-foundationalist. So if she is a hard absolutist, she would have to be so only from within the context of the relative field.

Barbara: Well, she can't be absolutist in any of those human senses, because those senses are intelligible to start with by virtue of their contrasts, by virtue of what they are not. So, from the field of the absolute in her special sense, she can be no absolutist.

Ronnie: So she's an absolutist and not an absolutist, depending upon the field from which you consider the question. I know what's coming, though. But before you accuse Nina of being contradictory, keep in mind that when you say she is both an absolutist and not absolutist, she is so in different senses of absolute.

Barbara: OK, Nina. You've been quiet while the rest of us have been discussing how to characterize your view. What do you think?

Nina: From the side of the absolute, to ask whether my view is absolutist in the senses you mentioned—that is, with regard to realism, universalism, or foundationalism—as I have said before, the question does not arise. It is a misplaced question.

Barbara: Why is it misplaced?

Nina: Because, insofar as the distinction between relativism and absolutism falls under the rubric of the relative, the idea of the absolute is relative. It is internal to a reference frame. It would be an absolute relativism. Yet Oneness cannot fall under any rubric. It is what it is. So, Oneness is neither relativist nor absolutist. The distinctions that would have allowed you to generate the question about the place of Oneness are misplaced. They drop out.

Barbara: So I guess we each have to choose whether we wish to see the matter from the side of the relativist, the absolutist, both, or neither.

Adam: Right—and we do want to answer the question whether one or any of those options is true.

Winding Down

Nina: Oh my. That question will start the discussion all over again.

Barbara: Maybe that's exactly what we should do at our next reunion. I wonder what we'll think about all this when we do meet again.

Adam: Well, if there's one thing that I've learned from these four absorbing days together, it's that even though I remain an absolutist, I now have plenty of new questions about it—such as what kind of absolutist I really am.

Ronnie: That's true for me too, Adam. There are so many different kinds of relativism, I need to think hard about which kind to embrace.

Barbara: You know, even though I may not have succeeded in getting the two of you to agree on some important things, Ronnie and Adam, maybe you have come a little closer together in your positions. At the same time, Nina, you've introduced me to a whole other way of thinking about these things—or, I should say—not thinking about them. I'm interested to see where that might lead.

Nina: All of your questions and objections have gotten me thinking about the path I have chosen. That's why I'm keen to hear what Geshe Samten will have to say about Tibetan Buddhism when Barbara and I go to Sarnath tomorrow morning.

Adam: I'm so much looking forward to all of us reconnecting at our next reunion when we can discuss these things further.

Barbara: It's getting late and I'd like to take one final boat ride up the Ganges early in the morning before leaving for Sarnath. You know, it's the site of Buddha's first sermon after he is supposed to have achieved enlightenment. I'm keen to learn more about the Buddhist idea of emptiness of inherent existence.

Nina: Before leaving let's make sure to see Mr. Shashank to thank him. He's been such a terrific host and guide.

Ronnie: Yes indeed. Meanwhile, Adam and I will need to get to the airport to make our connections to Chennai for their big Indian music festival. The plane is supposed to leave around noon and we need to be at the airport in plenty of time.

Barbara: Rest well. Tomorrow's a big day.

Adam: See you in the morning.

~

For Further Reading

Bernstein, Richard. *Beyond Objectivism and Relativism: Science, Hermeneutics, and Praxis*. Oxford: B. Blackwell, 1983.

Collingwood, R. G. *Essay on Metaphysics*. Oxford: Clarendon Press, 1940.

Hale, Steven, ed. *The Blackwell Companion to Relativism*. Oxford: B. Blackwell, 2011.

Hanna, Patricia, and Bernard Harrison. *Word and World: Practice and the Foundations of Language*. Cambridge: Cambridge University Press, 2004.

Harré, Rom, and Michael Krausz. *Varieties of Relativism*. Oxford: B. Blackwell, 1996.

Kant, Immanuel. *The Critique of Pure Reason*, edited and translated by Paul Geyer and Allen Wood. Cambridge: Cambridge University Press, 1998.

Kellenberger, James. *Moral Relativism: A Dialogue*. Lanham, Md.: Rowman & Littlefield, 2008.

Krausz, Michael, ed. *Relativism: A Contemporary Anthology*. Columbia University Press, 2010. See especially articles by Kwame Anthony Appiah, Simon Blackburn, Paul Boghossian, Nancy Cartwright, Donald Davidson, Catherine Elgin, Nelson Goodman, Gilbert Harman, David Hoy, David Lyons, Alasdair MacIntyre, Joseph Margolis, Jitendra Mohanty, Martha Nussbaum and Amartya Sen, Richard Rorty, Charles Taylor, and David Wong.

Kuhn, Thomas. *The Structure of Scientific Revolutions*. Chicago, Ill.: University of Chicago Press, 1970.

Margolis, Joseph. *The Flux of History and the Flux of Science*. Berkeley: University of California Press, 1993.

McCormack, Peter J., ed. *Starmaking*. Cambridge, Mass.: MIT Press, 1996. See articles by Nelson Goodman, C. G. Hempel, Hilary Putnam, and Israel Scheffler.

Mohanty, Jitendra. *The Self and Its Other*. New Delhi: Oxford University Press, 2000.

Popper, Karl. *Conjectures and Refutations: The Growth of Scientific Knowledge.* London and New York: Routledge and Kegan Paul, 2002.

Whorf, Benjamin Lee. *Language, Thought, and Reality.* Cambridge, Mass.: MIT Press, 1956.

Wittgenstein, Ludwig. *Tractatus Logico-Philosophicus*, edited by David Pears and Brian McGuinness. London: Routledge, 1961.

Wittgenstein, Ludwig. *Philosophical Investigations.* Oxford: B. Blackwell, 1953.

Zimmer, Heinrich. *Philosophies of India.* Princeton, N.J.: Princeton University Press, 1989.

~

Index

absolutism: hard and soft a., 81, 82;
negation of relativism, 64; relative
a., 35–40, 85, 87; relativism and a.,
oppositions between, 85; strands
of absolutism, 63–65, 67, 69–71,
73, 75, 77, 79, 81, 83, 86, 122.
See also foundationalism; realism;
universalism
absolute relativism, 35, 36, 38–40, 54,
85, 87, 99, 102, 123
adjudication between reference frames,
10, 11, 16, 18, 23, 25–30, 32, 36, 42,
55, 77
Atman, 21, 27, 60, 61, 80, 92
Anatman, 21
awareness, 110, 111
axiomatic statements, 39, 54–6

beliefs, 4, 11, 21, 23, 24; reference
frames, b. in contrast to, 17, 18
bivalence vs. multivalence, 44, 45
bliss(fulness), 103–5
Buddhism, 2, 19, 20, 60, 61, 79, 119,
120; B. versus Hinduism, 80; Tibetan
B., 60, 124

Christianity, 59, 60, 78
cognitivists, 48
commonality, 19, 21, 82
consciousness, 101, 102, 105, 119

differentiation, 9, 25–29, 80, 92,
93, 95–97, 115; undifferentiated
Atman/Oneness, 35, 103, 104, 123;
undifferentiated "stuff," 17, 33–37,
44, 88, 100
diversity, 11, 74; reference frames, d. of,
14, 15, 33, 34
domains, 45–50, 52, 57, 58, 60–62, 81;
reconcilliation of absolutism and
relativism by d., 45–8
dualism, 93, 95, 96, 102, 108, 110, 111,
114, 116, 121, 122; language, d. of,
112

emptiness, 9, 21, 76, 79, 124
epistemic vs. ontic, 37, 38, 40–42,
65–67, 70, 78, 79

fact(s) of the matter, 3, 6, 7, 9, 11–13,
17, 19, 20–23, 25, 31, 33, 37, 39, 40,

~

About the Author

Michael Krausz is Milton C. Nahm Professor of Philosophy at Bryn Mawr College. He is the author of *Rightness and Reasons: Interpretation in Cultural Practices*, *Varieties of Relativism* (with Rom Harré), *Limits of Rightness*, *Interpretation and Transformation: Explorations in Art and the Self*, and *Dialogues on Relativism, Absolutism, and Beyond: Four Days in India*. Krausz is also contributing editor or co-editor of eleven volumes on relativism, rationality, interpretation, cultural identity, creativity, and related themes. Andreea Deciu Ritivoi edited a festschrift on his philosophical work, entitled *Interpretation and Its Objects: Studies in the Philosophy of Michael Krausz*.

As a visual artist, Michael Krausz has had thirty-three solo and duo exhibitions in galleries in the United States, United Kingdom, and India. As a musician, Krausz is the founding Artistic Director and Conductor of the Great Hall Chamber Orchestra, comprised of forty-two young professional musicians. He teaches Aesthetics at the Curtis Institute of Music in Philadelphia.

CPSIA information can be obtained at www.ICGtesting.com
Printed in the USA
BVOW022036091111

275613BV00003BA/1/P